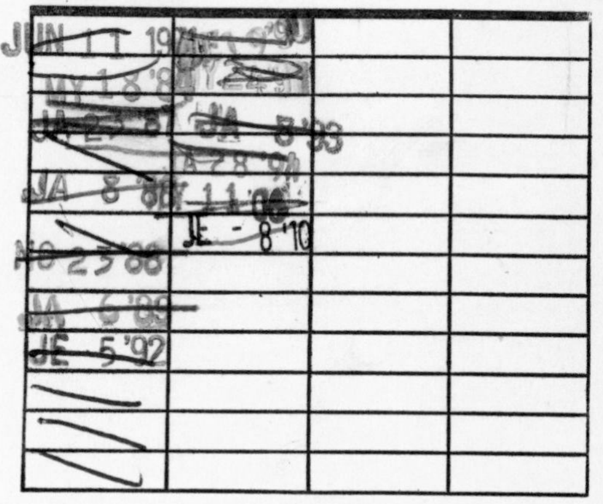

WAR, PEACE, AND THE VIET CONG

DOUGLAS PIKE

WAR, PEACE, AND THE VIET CONG

THE M.I.T. PRESS

Massachusetts Institute of Technology
Cambridge, Massachusetts, and London, England

Set in Linotype Granjon
and printed by The Heffernan Press
Bound in the United States of America by The Colonial Press

Library of Congress catalog card number: 70-83403

A PERSONAL PREFACE

Vietnam defies simplification. At the vortex, Saigon, the complexity is greatest, the view most personal. Even after eight years one cannot leave Vietnam with any Great Truth Concluded unless one is simple-minded or the servant of some interest other than truth (we've had more than our share of both). I flew out of Saigon dozens of times during the war and always, at take-off, with the same thoughts:

¶ That in my latest stay I'd had no increment of wisdom, that at best I had managed to maintain a cool objective view, suspecting all the time that objectivity may reflect, not sagacity, only uncertainty.

¶ That once again I was leaving behind a place of pluses and minuses, of goods and bads (all, I cheerfully admit, measured by my own yardstick), of paradoxes and imponderables, leaving again with the tinge of sadness that comes in moments of reflection on the plight of the Vietnamese people, on one's own sins of omission, on the passage of time.

¶ That beyond a few facts about Vietnam that I cart around like an attaché case, all else hangs in a smog of relativity. One concludes that to leave heartened or sympathetic or revengeful or full of despair depends only slightly on where you were, for how long, or what you experienced in Vietnam; it indicates only baggage that you brought with you:

> Who was that early sodbuster in Kansas? He leaned at the gatepost and studied the horizon and figured what corn might do next year and tried to calculate why God ever made the grasshopper and why two days of hot winds smother the life out of a stand of wheat and why there was such a spread between what he got for grain and the price quoted in Chicago and New York. Drove up a newcomer in a covered wagon: "What kind of folks live around here?" "Well, stranger, what kind of folks was there in the country you come from?" "Well, they was mostly a low-down, lying, thieving, gossiping, backbiting lot of people." "Well, I guess, stranger, that's about the kind of folks you'll find around here." And the dusty gray stranger had just about blended into the dusty gray cottonwoods in a clump on the horizon when another newcomer drove up: "What kind of folks live around here?" "Well, stranger, what kind of folks was there in the country you come from?" "Well, they was mostly a decent, hardworking, lawabiding, friendly lot of people." "Well, I guess, stranger, that's about the kind of folks you'll find around here." And the second wagon moved off and blended with the dusty gray cottonwoods on the horizon while the early sodbuster leaned at his gatepost and tried to figure why two days of hot winds smother the life out of a nice stand of wheat.[1]

Raw opinion on Vietnam is cheap and largely worthless. Even straight facts are of limited value. Of course, to understand Vietnam it is necessary to collect data, but the fumbling comes in isolating important fact from the welter of trivia, in distilling the data into meaning. The materials consist of past and present events, our opinion of them, the ideal of what might be. The task of those of us who write about Vietnam is to relate the reality of the war to the logic of our experience. Herein lies the gulf. Vietnam has become

[1] Carl Sandburg, *The People, Yes* (New York: Harcourt, Brace and Company, 1936).

the great intellectual tragedy of our times. Why this is so I do not understand. Living in Vietnam for eight years has contributed nothing to my enlightenment. The story of Vietnam has not been told, not even its beginnings. Perhaps it must be told from somewhere else. Perhaps nonfiction is the wrong medium. My greatest despair is that the story may never be told the way it was. Even as I write, I must admit that my strongest feeling toward Vietnam remains puzzlement. Such, perhaps, is the truth for all of us. In the past two years I have traveled 150,000 miles, talking to people in 47 countries about Vietnam. Most, I find, frankly don't care much about Vietnam; they come to hear me out of curiosity, remain to ask questions out of courtesy. I have never encountered a single truly hostile audience. The predominant reaction of the overwhelming majority of those to whom I've talked has been genuine confusion; they are puzzled about why the war goes on for so long, what America is doing there, why nothing moves as common sense would dictate. This view was exquisitely condensed by a question from an Indian in Calcutta (who obviously had been influenced by American English) who rose and with great dignity asked, not flippantly or provocatively, but in the intensely serious manner that the Bengali can best muster: "Sir, what's with Vietnam?"

That, I felt, was the ultimate question. What's with Vietnam? Now that we have the question, I thought, if only we had the ultimate answer.

This volume deals with Vietnam and its transition from the strife of war to the strife of peace. It focuses chiefly on the strategy, the interests, and the objectives of those whom the world calls the Viet Cong. Chapter One lists the contenders in the struggle and describes their basic objectives.

Chapter Two deals with context, the social and political milieu in which the struggle is being fought. Then, in Chapter Three, I attempt to suggest the alternate directions events in Vietnam may take. Chapter Four, the heart of this book, is concerned with the major strategic options open. Finally, Chapter Five adds some summary comments on short-term prospects and long-term possibilities. The touchstone throughout is rational strategy and doctrine. The primary orientation is that it is best to view Vietnam not as a war that requires victory but as a problem that requires solution.

This book is intended for those who are seriously interested in the Vietnam struggle. It is not a recapitulation of recent events in Vietnam and, in fact, deliberately seeks not to duplicate basic reporting of recent years. Rather it is an attempt to provide a factual background for understanding Vietnam at the moment and for events following in the next few years as peace gradually returns. The focus is on objectives and strategies of contending forces, and therefore, the author hopes, the book will remain useful regardless of the zigzag of specific events in Vietnam.

A word on sources. Most of the ideas and data contained here come from the rather candid published statements by the North Vietnamese and the National Liberation Front leaders; these have been more valuable than all other sources combined. The second most important source has been the tons of documents picked up by American and Vietnamese troops on the battlefield in the course of military operations; several thousand of the most important of these, including ones used in this book, have been microfilmed and catalogued and are available though the Center for International Studies at M.I.T. and the Southeast Asia Program at Cornell University (unfortunately for interested Americans, most are without English translations).

I am a United States Foreign Service Officer making a career in the United States Information Agency. This book was written privately, on my own time. Any views expressed here are mine and should not be interpreted as reflecting the views of the U.S. Government. This does not mean, I should hope, that they are not shared by many of my colleagues within the government.

It is beyond the ken of any man to see down the road into Vietnam's future beyond a few weeks. Beware of those who claim to be able to do so. Because we cannot see ahead, we tend to despair that the war will never end. This sense of endlessness in wartime is neither new nor unique. I was in New Guinea in 1944 and remember hearing of a "hundred-year war" against Japan seriously predicted and convincingly argued. In Seoul in 1952 I recall a dinner at which a French general maintained that the Korean war had to go on indefinitely because "it couldn't logically end." That we cannot see the end to a war is not the same as that there is no end. Wars do end, thank God, and often sooner than we have a right to expect.

Saigon, Vietnam
December 1, 1968

Douglas Pike

CONTENTS

WAR, PEACE, AND THE VIET CONG

CHAPTER ONE

CONTENDERS AND OBJECTIVES

Although some are more important than others, eight separate forces are responsible for the current Vietnam scene, and all eight must be taken into consideration in accounting for present-day Vietnam or anticipating its tomorrow. Each impinges on the other seven, and the permutations of the relationships are enough to make the mind boggle. It is precisely for this reason that Vietnam, the most complex condition of the twentieth century, defies simplification.

The eight forces are: the National Liberation Front of South Vietnam (NLF), including its armed force now called the People's Liberation Armed Force (PLAF); the People's Revolutionary Party (PRP) or Communist Party of South Vietnam;[1] the newly created Vietnamese Alliance of National, Democratic, and Peace Forces (referred to throughout this book as the Alliance); the Democratic Re-

[1] These two, the NLF and the PRP (or three if PLAF is considered a separate entity), generally are what is meant by the term *Viet Cong*. This is an imprecise term but one, rightly or wrongly, which now is in wide and permanent use. *Viet Cong* is a contraction of *Viet Nam Cong San*, meaning Vietnamese Communist. As was the case in my first book, *Viet Cong*, I have employed the term in the title so as to indicate what the book is about, but I have not used it in the text; in both cases, *Viet Cong* has the broadest possible definition.

public of Vietnam (DRV), that is, North Vietnam and its armed force, the People's Army of Vietnam (PAVN); Communist China; the Soviet Union; the Republic or Government of Vietnam (GVN) and its armed force (RVNAF); the United States and the Allied or Pacific Ocean powers with troops in Vietnam, namely, South Korea, Thailand, the Philippines, Australia, and New Zealand.

We begin by examining each of the eight in terms of composition and specific objective, that is, the *who* and the *what* of the Vietnam war contenders.

The National Liberation Front

The National Liberation Front of South Vietnam[2] is a front organization in the technical sense but one that, unlike most front organizations elsewhere, has a military structure. The front itself is composed of some twenty sociopolitical organizations and has a membership, as of early 1969, of about 300,000 (of whom some 40,000 are full-time cadres). The civilian organizations within the NLF are of two basic types, administrative and functional. The administrative liberation association is conceived as a quasi government, a hierarchy running from the national NLF Central Committee down through a series of intervening central committees to the village liberation association committee. The functional liberation association exists essentially only at the village level. The major ones are the Farmers' Liberation Association, the Workers' Liberation Association

[2] The most commonly employed form of the term by both sides. In Vietnamese it is *Mat Tran Dan Toc Giai Phong Mien Nam Vietnam.* Literally it means "Front of Racial Nationals for the Liberation of the Region That Is Southern Vietnam." Frequently it is encountered in print as National Front for Liberation of South Vietnam or NFLSV.

(chiefly in the rubber tapper villages), the Women's Liberation Association, the Youth Liberation Association, the Student Liberation Association, and the Cultural Liberation Association (chiefly schoolteachers, religious figures, and such intellectuals as exist in the village). In addition there are two kept political parties, the Radical Socialist Party and the Democratic Party of South Vietnam; a series of special-interest (*van hoi*) groups, such as veterans' organizations or the Patriotic and Democratic Journalists' Association; and finally, externally oriented groups, such as the Afro-Asian People's Solidarity Committee. The paramount member of the NLF, as it states in its own publications, is the People's Revolutionary Party (considered later). The administrative liberation association structure is elite, tightly disciplined, and relatively easy for cadres to control. The functional liberation association structure is more broadly based and more sociopolitical than governmental. The front formed by these groups, however, predates the groups themselves. The NLF thus reversed the usual order for the formation of a united front—as, for example, the Popular Front of Europe in the 1930's—for instead of beginning with the organizations and creating the front, the NLF began with the front and created the organizations. When the NLF was founded, on December 20, 1960, it was correctly labeled by the world as a phantom edifice, for it existed only on paper. But as the months passed, the dephantomizing process went forward, the skeleton was fleshed out, and the NLF became a reality.

The People's Liberation Armed Force, prior to 1966 known as the Liberation Army of the NLF, consists of two elements, a Full Military Force and a Paramilitary Force. The Full Military, usually referred to as the Main Force, or "hard hats" (because of the fiberboard Viet Minh helmets worn by the troops), numbers about 60,000, while the Paramilitary or guerrilla force numbers around 180,000 persons including women. The Paramilitary Force is of two types: the Regional or Territorial Guerrilla unit, the classic sort of guerrilla band, living in a remote area, making its forays, supported by villagers in the area; and the Local Guerrilla, also of a classic type, the part-time fighter who farms by day and blows up bridges by night.

Political power, all the political power if possible, quite clearly represents the NLF's objective. It regards itself as the sole, genuine, legitimate representative of the South Vietnamese people and labels the Saigon government "rebel" and illegitimate. The language it speaks, although militant and sloganized, is the language of government and politics. In its most authoritative pronouncement of objective, a 7,500-word document issued as a program in 1967,[3] the NLF listed its four major planks as: (1) to save the nation (that is, save it "from the U.S. aggressors"); (2) to work for reunification of the fatherland; (3) to build an independent, democratic, peaceful, neutral, and prosperous Vietnam, and (4) to apply a foreign policy of "peace and neutrality." Plank number three was broken down into fourteen "concrete policies":

1. To establish a progressive government.
2. To develop the economy.
3. To institute land reform.
4. To promote education, culture, science, technology, and public health.
5. To improve working conditions.

[3] For a discussion of these policy pronouncements see Douglas Pike, *Viet Cong: The Organization and Techniques of the National Liberation Front of South Vietnam* (Cambridge, Mass.: The M.I.T. Press, 1966).

6. To develop the armed forces.
7. To provide veterans' benefits.
8. To provide social welfare benefits.
9. To establish equality of the sexes.
10. To integrate minorities.
11. To guarantee religious freedom.
12. To implement an amnesty program.
13. To protect the rights of absent Vietnamese.
14. To protect the rights of foreigners in Vietnam.

Ho Chi Minh has described the aims of the NLF in these terms:

> The program of the South Viet Nam National Liberation Front clearly specified its principal aims. These are: to struggle against aggressive U.S. imperialism, to liberate the South, to achieve independence, democracy, peace, and neutrality, and advance step by step toward the reunification of the country. The South Viet Nam National Front for Liberation is an organization of the patriotic movement, set up by the mass of the people. The front is the leader, the organizer of the South Vietnamese people's struggle against U.S. imperialism to recover national independence. The Front is the only genuine representative of the South Vietnamese people. It is the sacred duty of the whole people of Viet Nam to support the South Vietnamese people's liberation struggle, waged under the leadership of the National Front for Liberation. We [DRV] respect the policies of the Front and hold that the two zones must take their respective characteristics into account, understand each other, restore normal relations between them and gradually achieve national reunification. Viet Nam is one. The Vietnamese are one people. Our entire people have the duty of opposing foreign aggression and defending the Fatherland.[4]

[4] An interview with a London *Daily Worker* correspondent as reprinted in the North Vietnamese magazine *Viet Nam Courier,* July 15, 1965.

The basic characteristics of the NLF are these: use of the united-front organization as a means of establishing a mass base of support; heavy use of communication of ideas to foment social strife; harnessing of the energies of the people through the use of a social myth; utilization of the divisive Marxist class struggle theses; and employment of specialized military action, usually selective in nature and psychological in intent. The NLF, as of early 1969, had about 750,000 hardcore supporters out of a nation of 18.9 million; this includes the 300,000 civilian members of the various NLF organizations as well as the members of the PLAF. At one time it was supported by many more Vietnamese, with its pinnacle of popularity reached in mid-1963 when President Ngo Dinh Diem was locked in combat with Vietnamese Buddhist organizations. At that time perhaps half the population of South Vietnam at least tacitly supported the NLF. But the rise of militant Buddhism broke the monopoly of government opposition that the NLF had held, and for that reason as well as others its popularity began to decline. As of late 1968, political observers in Saigon believed 10 to 15 per cent was the most support that the NLF could claim, which included the hardcore supporters as well as sympathizers. The support that the NLF has known in the past, however, has been not for ideological, but for social reasons. Social pressure caused a young man to join the ranks of the NLF Army. For a long period, social pressure caused him to remain loyal. Parts of rural Vietnam have been under tight NLF control for a generation.[5] In these villages the local leaders originally were obeyed and even protected. The NLF in the past several years has steadily lost the close identification with the people that

[5] And before the NLF, the Viet Minh.

marked its earlier days in Vietnam. These people, mostly villagers, became disenchanted with the cause because of the compulsory draft, which takes young men far from their home villages; increased and never-ending financial demands; a growing coerciveness in the system; and inability of the PLAF to defend them against attack. Increasingly stringent NLF regulations also have alienated villagers. Without doubt, the leaders' paranoic preoccupation with "spies" has had a deadly effect. When Allied troops have freed prisoners from NLF "jails," they have heard bone-chilling stories of "justice" in the villages. Cadres are now authorized to shoot villagers on the spot. There is widespread use of a new institution in South Vietnam NLF-controlled areas: the thought-reform session. Although NLF-villager relations have deteriorated to the point where the average villager's attitude ranges from strong dislike to outright hatred, the Front continues to be supported by the villagers and receives from them money, food, group labor, or young men. The villagers supply the NLF because of threats and coercion. The size of the unwilling support group may range as high as 40 per cent of the total rural population. Therefore, the NLF, despite growing hostility, remains viable. The explanation of why this is so, why support comes from basically hostile people, lies in the fact that the NLF's strength through the years has been organizational. It became a power not because of the attraction of communism (or some variant of Marxism-Leninism, such as Maoism), not because of grievances against the Government of Vietnam, not because of frustrated aspirations, not because of poverty. Although all of these conditions exist to some degree in Vietnam, none serves to explain the power of the NLF. Only superb organization at the lowest level can account for its strength. That there is no great ideological force behind the NLF should not be difficult to grasp. An organization such as the French Foreign Legion, in its day a highly effective fighting force, had no ideological engine driving it ahead. The secret of the NLF is superb organization.

The NLF represents a political process — perhaps political weapon would be a more apt term — new in degree if not in kind to the world of political activism. It is a powerful technique blending politics with violence. Its essence, more organizational than doctrinal, is old-fashioned only in that it is directed toward the orthodox goal of political control or political power. Many terms have been used in assembling definitions and descriptions of this phenomenon: revolutionary guerrilla warfare, united frontism, national salvation struggle, protracted conflict, creative violence, Maoism, and wars of national liberation. Despite superficial appearances, it is chiefly a *political* process, with the entirety being far more political than military. Yet even this distinction, between military and nonmilitary activity, is misleading, for one of the unique characteristics of the NLF is the blurring of the line between the political and the military, between war and peace. It rests on the assumption that it is necessary to ignore traditional political roles, that new paths in politics must be cut, new types of political behavior developed, and that the past must not be built on but must be ignored. There is a totality about it not usually associated with the word "politics." It demands undivided involvement. It is a way of life. Since it seeks not to adjust the political machine but to smash it, the NLF is in tune with the nihilism of the second half of the twentieth century, the spirit of rebellion for its own sake, the blanket condemnation of all Establishment, the drive to harness the alienated, and the injection of violence into the forefront of political change regardless of cost.

What the NLF would do substantively if it achieved power remains a moot question, one that even a candid leader probably cannot answer with much specificity. During the past eight years the leadership has been preoccupied with doctrinal problems—how to come to power rather than what to do with power once achieved. When an ex-NLF member is asked why he fought, his answer invariably is cast in terms of political virtues: to achieve justice, democracy, and economic opportunity, to end corruption, to "return the government to the people," and so on. He believes in these virtues and wants political power in order to make them reality. The NLF's public pronouncements, such as the stated objectives cited earlier, are almost meaningless for political assessment because they are the goals of the GVN as well; for that matter, what government anywhere in the world does not claim to stand for progress, economic development, promotion of education, culture, science, technology, public health, and so on? In policy as well the NLF seeks to define the enemy in the narrowest terms possible. Its agit-prop cadres speaking in the villages offer appeals far more bourgeois than proletarian: landlords are not evil as such, but are divided into "oppressive" landlords and "patriotic" landlords (the difference being whether they are willing to cooperate with the NLF). In any case the NLF, regardless of the war's outcome, will be dominated by Northerners with never a chance to exhibit their true selves. The Southerners no longer direct the organization, nor have they since the "regularization" or communization of the Front was completed in 1964. Control now is in the hands of the Tonkinese or Northerners. About half of the 40,000 civilian NLF cadres previously noted are so-called "pure" Northerners, as opposed to the "regrouped" Southerner (that is, the Southerner who went North during Operation Exodus in 1954) or the Cochin Chinese Southerner; a "pure" Northerner is a person from North Vietnam who plans to return to North Vietnam, whose family is in North Vietnam, whose career is bound up with North Vietnam, and who therefore is basically loyal to the Northern objective of unification rather than the NLF objective of political power. If the NLF ever were to win in South Vietnam, it would be these Northerners who would assume the actual mantle of power, and their subsequent decisions would be made on the basis of DRV interests rather than Southern interests.

The year 1968 saw a sharp reduction in the importance of the NLF in the struggle in the South. With one exception (the Tet offensive) all the major battles of the year were fought by PAVN troops, not NLF troops. The battle of Khe Sanh, for example, involved three PAVN divisions; there were no NLF troops as such at Khe Sanh, although some NLF "fillers" were there in PAVN units. The NLF also came to count for less politically during the year, its monopoly on "legitimacy" broken by the creation of the Alliance (see p. 18); no longer could it claim to be the "sole legitimate representative" of the South Vietnamese people.

The People's Revolutionary Party

Until January 1962 the Communist Party in South Vietnam was known as the Southern Branch of the Vietnam Workers' Party (*Dang Lao Dong*), but at that time it was decided to abolish the Southern Branch and replace it with what came to be known as the People's Revolutionary Party of South Vietnam.[6] The decision was made for several reasons, according to Party members who have since left the movement. First, the leadership felt that the tasks of the two parties were different (the Party in the North was to build communism, while the Southerners were to liberate the South), and that different tasks required different organizational structures. Also, the leadership in Hanoi believed that its followers in the South needed more support, as apparently they did; *hoi chanh* (ex-NLF) say that during the 1960–1962 period many Marxists in the South suffered from a sense of ideological isolation, a feeling of being cut off from the main stream of Communist thought and surrounded by nonbelievers, that these feelings developed into severe cases of doubt and indecision, forcing Hanoi to shore up the ideological underpinnings in the South by strengthening the apparatus. Stronger communism also was required, from the DRV viewpoint, to forestall possible NLF separatism, the DRV *bête-noire* that the Soviets had been warning them about. As part of the Sino-Soviet debate the Soviets had long argued that, in general, guerrillas are a poor means of putting Communists into power, for too often they begin as Communists and end as nationalists. Whether Hanoi took this advice completely is not known, but it did act to guard against separatism in the NLF ranks.

The PRP never denied in its public statements that it was communistic. Neither did it deny that it was much more

[6] In Vietnamese *Dang Nhan Dan Cach Mang (Viet Nam)*; for reasons never understandable to Westerners, the Communists in Vietnam avoid the term "communism" (*cong*). The North Vietnam Communist Party's official name (Workers' Party—*Dang Lao Dong*) does not contain the term, nor has it since the abolition of the Indochinese Communist Party in 1945. In speeches and public statements DRV officials avoid the use of the word *cong* where possible.

than simply a member of the NLF. Originally the PRP's stated role in the NLF was somewhat limited. It would assert, for example, that it was the "engine of the Revolution," the "vanguard" of the NLF, the "soul" of the NLF, also that it had no official ties with Communist parties or governments elsewhere beyond the "fraternal ties of communism." In short, the PRP claimed that it was the leader and the central organ of the NLF, which also included non-Communists, and that it was a Vietnamese nationalistic Communist organization. In 1965 this changed. A typical new characterization of the PRP came in an article in the North Vietnamese theoretical journal *Hoc Tap* titled "The Vietnamese People's Revolutionary Party and Its Historic Mission of Liberating the South":[7]

> The partisans of Marxism-Leninism are in fact the soul of the NLFSV. . . .
>
> The experiences of the world and our country's revolution have shown that in order to win the greatest success the national democratic revolution must be led by a workers' revolutionary party. . . . The partisans of Marxism-Leninism in the South have clearly noted the need for a thoroughly revolutionary party to act as a vanguard force for the southern revolution. . . .
>
> The PRP is a revolutionary party of the working class in South Vietnam, a Marxist-Leninist Party. It has applied in a creative manner the principles of Marxism-Leninism to the concrete situation of the South in order to set forth correct revolutionary policies, lines and methods. . . .
>
> The PRP maintains that the revolutionary struggle of the southern people must necessarily use the revolutionary violence of the masses to . . . advance toward smashing the reactionary government and replace it by a genuinely revolutionary government. . . . Straying from this path can lead only to a failure.

[7] Hong Vu, "The Vietnamese PRP and Its Historic Mission in Liberating the South," *Hoc Tap* (Hanoi, January 1966).

The PRP began not only admitting but vaunting both its Communist nature and the paramountcy in the NLF. The PRP does this within Vietnam, even in public statements, but not externally. Prior to about mid-1966 the PRP structure ran from a central committee down to and including the district level, but not into the village as an organizational structure. In 1966 the *apparat* was extended all the way to the village by order of a PRP Central Committee directive that overhauled basic PRP-NLF relations. The order had the effect of putting Communists, as Party members, into positions of direct overt control of the insurgency. While regularization or communization of the struggle had been underway for several years, the order completed the process. Its objectives were to build up the numerical strength of the Party—and the leadership seemed more interested in numbers than quality—and to push the individual Party cadre and Party member forward into stronger, more prominent leadership roles. Membership in late 1968 was estimated at about 75,000, including members of the PRP Youth League, the junior organization. Almost all of the 40,000 NLF cadres mentioned earlier also are PRP members, and, as noted, about half are Northerners. Among the practical results of the changes were an increased importance of the PRP and a corresponding decline of the NLF. Quite probably, future historians of the Vietnam war will record as one of its most important milestones the rise of the PRP and the shift to overt Communist leadership. It was a decision made because it was forced. The leadership became convinced that only by this means could the Front remain viable. The need was for a tighter, more centralized organization, more effective leadership, more dedicated cadres, and for the discipline, experience, and knowledge that only the Party could supply. Also needed was more ideology, something to explain events to the faithful and provide them with a sense of certitude. Probably the changes in the directive did yield some of the results that the leadership sought. Perhaps the changes were beneficial as far as the Party members were concerned. But they had a strongly negative effect on indigenous Southerners in the NLF, especially the old-time cadres. Arriving *hoi chanh* began to tell interviewers that the "revolution has been betrayed," and for that reason they left the NLF ranks.

Organizationally the PRP employs directives and other official instructions from the Lao Dong or North Vietnamese Communist Party; it issues few documents in its own name.

Its official platform, issued at its founding in January 1962 and widely distributed throughout South Vietnam, listed ten points for which it stood:

1. We will overthrow the Ngo Dinh Diem government and form a national democratic coalition government.
2. We will carry out a program involving extension of democratic liberties, general amnesty for political detainees, abolition of agrovilles and resettlement centers, abolition of special military tribunal law and other undemocratic laws.
3. We will abolish the economic monopoly of the U.S. and its henchmen, protect domestically made products, promote development of the economy, and allow forced evacuees from North Vietnam to return to their place of birth.
4. We will reduce land rent and prepare for land reform.
5. We will eliminate U.S. cultural enslavement and depravity and build nationalistic progressive culture and education.
6. We will abolish the system of American military advisers and close all foreign military bases in Vietnam.
7. We will establish equality between men and women and among different nationalities and recognize the autonomous rights of the national minorities in the country.
8. We will pursue a foreign policy of peace and will establish

diplomatic relations with all countries that respect the independence and sovereignty of Vietnam.

9. We will re-establish normal relations between North and South as a first step toward peaceful reunification of the country.

10. We will oppose aggressive wars and actively defend world peace.

In April 1962 the PRP Central Committee issued what might be considered its foreign policy platform. It denounced the United States for "waging aggressive war" in South Vietnam; it thanked the Soviet Union, Communist China, and the bloc nations for supporting its cause; it urged all "peace-loving peoples" of the world to support the Vietnamese revolution; it urged the American people to demonstrate opposition to their government's policy in Vietnam; it denounced the British government for its stand on Vietnam; and it hinted that unless the Americans left Vietnam, it would call on the DRV, China, and the Soviet Union to come to its aid.

The objective of the PRP members is the more or less stated objective of Communists everywhere, namely the advancement of communism, which admittedly can be variously defined.[8] A PRP cadre training manual, dated October 1965, described the PRP's policies and goals thus:

> The Party [objective] . . . is to overthrow imperialism, colonialism, and feudalism, to build a life of peace, prosperity, and happiness without oppression and extortion. . . . Once indepen-

[8] The average PRP member would agree that "the history of all hitherto existing societies is the history of the class conflict." And he would say he believes in historical determinism, even if not sure of the term, that inevitably feudalism gives way to socialism phasing into communism, the key word being "inevitably." Even in this day of Communist polycentricism it seems safe to assert that most Communists throughout the world regard the class conflict and historical determination doctrines as being bedrock Marxism-Leninism and to deny them is to deny communism. See Chapter Five, pp. 176–177.

dence is obtained, the next step is unification, constructed and consolidated in every way to make the country powerful and rich, a stronghold of peace. Then will come the social reorganization, along Socialist-Communist principles, without land demarcation, cooperating in rural electrification, re-education of individuals, nationalization of private property, cultural and scientific education for everyone, progressing day by day to better and better things in all fields. . . . To prevent a return of parisitism and laziness that characterized the old regime, we will follow the Socialist principle of rewarding each according to his ability. We shall all live together intimately in the great Socialist family. . . . Once Vietnam is reunited and Socialism created, the Party will then continue to lead the people toward the establishment of communism. Communism will be practiced as it is in the Soviet Union. Factories, mines, fields, and all other land will be the common ownership of all the people. . . . Also, helping other small weak countries to struggle against imperialism and rid the world of conflict and to help provide everyone with freedom, legality, warmth, food, and happiness.

Something of the nature of the PRP is indicated by the PRP Party Pledge:

With the aid of Party members I have come to understand that the Party exists to achieve a national democratic revolution to pave the way to a Socialist and then Communist society. The Party's mission is to serve the proletariat, always struggling for their rights and privileges. It is the proletariat's destiny to be the vanguard of the Revolution, in both thought and deed. The Party strives to serve the people and their aspirations. *Kiem thao* [self-criticism] sessions strengthen our class consciousness, our solidarity, our will to fight.

I understand these things. I know and subscribe to the principles, directives, and purposes of the Party.

I hereby petition to become a member of the Party and pledge I will accept Party discipline and pay Party dues.

I expect to receive Party education so as to be able to advance the Revolution and fulfill the missions entrusted to me by the Party. I recognize the honor bestowed by admission to the Party and stand willing to sacrifice all for the Party and the Revolution. In making this pledge I enhance my own life.

Once a Party member I pledge:

To be faithful to the Party and respect its many achievements.

To follow Party directives all designed to ensure the success of the Revolution.

To study Marxism-Leninism to strengthen my revolutionary consciousness and logic.

To strive to complete every mission assigned to me by the Party.

To engage in *kiem thao* sessions so as to improve my relations with the proletariat, strengthen the Party, and improve myself.

To protect the Party's honor and good name.[9]

The Party is particularly insistent on loyalty to the objective of unification and has made faith in this goal a requirement for all comrades. It appears to have been successful. Only Communist *hoi chanh* describe geographic regionalism in Vietnam (see the discussion in Chapter Two) as "bourgeois sentimentality," although some admit to interrogators that they have had difficulty in exorcising the attitude.

PRP cadres, especially in earlier years, were told to mute the Socialist-Communist nature of the organization where it was appropriate, as for example in an area with a heavy concentration of Catholic Vietnamese. Strangely, however, in outer trappings such as flags, the Communist imprint is firm. The PRP flag is a red field with a white hammer and sickle in the center; the PRP Youth League flag is a red field with three yellow stars in the center and a white hammer and sickle at the upper right. The PRP is a Janus-faced organization. In the South it insists to the Vietnamese people

[9] This is the so-called "blood oath" of the PRP, often signed with solemn ceremony; the oath text often varies slightly. The one cited here is circa 1966.

that it is not Communist but Marxist-Leninist, indicating philosophic but not political allegiance and implying some sort of national communism. And it asserts internal control of the NLF. Internally and in the North the DRV characterizes the PRP as a vanguard Marxist-Leninist organization, indicating that it is in the mainstream of the world-wide Communist movement, both spiritually and materially connected to the North Vietnamese, the DRV government, and the Lao Dong. This is alliance communism. Regardless of its ideological image, there now is no ambiguity in the NLF-PRP relationship. The NLF is dominated by the PRP as an organization, by PRP goals, and by PRP cadres. So long as their two objectives — political power as the objective of the NLF and unification of the two Vietnams as the objective of the PRP — run parallel, the NLF-PRP machine will remain viable. But once the crossroads of choice are reached, then a rupture within the NLF is virtually inevitable. The size of the breakaway NLF force will be determined chiefly by the success of PRP cadres between now and the day of the future split, in weeding out potential deviationists.

The Alliance of National, Democratic, and Peace Forces

The PAVN-NLF Winter–Spring Campaign of 1967–1968 spawned a host of new political and quasi-military organizations in South Vietnam, all integrated, in varying degrees, into the NLF and the PRP. For a few months after the launching of the lunar new year (or Tet) offensive in February 1968, the proliferation of these groups was overwhelming. Alliances, regional fronts, "uprising" committees, political associations, revolutionary councils, federations of "peace-loving Buddhist soldiers," all churned out a welter of manifestoes, communiqués, action reports, "solemn declarations," and so on, as if the intent were chiefly to confound and bewilder foreign correspondents, academic researchers, and intelligence analysts in Saigon.

Gradually these NLF-sponsored organizations began to sort themselves out. One cluster, it was clear, consisted of proselyting organizations (called *binh van* in NLF terminology) designed to contribute to the Tet military campaign. A second cluster called People's Revolutionary Councils were designed to administer towns and cities temporarily after victory, employing a commune concept like the original Paris commune or the Shanghai commune of the 1920's. The third cluster was made up of negotiational front organizations.

The first cluster, the proselyting groups, employed various communicational, psychological, and political devices to induce — at the maximum — desertion by South Vietnamese soldiers or defection by GVN civil servants or — at the minimum — a lowering of the soldiers' will to fight or of the civil servants' dedication. This was a direct auxiliary contribution to the military offensive.

The second cluster was designed to be the precursor of a new revolutionary government, a bridge to facilitate the eventual amalgamation of the Southern and DRV administrative structures. These did not last in the cities after the Tet offensive, of course, because the PLAF could not prevail there; but they did continue to appear, at least in public reference,[10] in the more remote areas where they were

[10] In June 1968 Radio Liberation claimed that some 600 of the village councils had been created (out of a total of 2,500 villages in South Vietnam), which was approximately the same number of villages under NLF control. Radio Hanoi broadcasts at the same time, however, were using the figure of 100 village councils.

known as People's Liberation Councils or People's Liberation Committees, or collectively as People's Administration. After the failure of the PLAF to seize and hold the cities, the leadership decided to use the mechanism of the newly created people's council structure in overhauling administration in the NLF-controlled areas. Village administration was reorganized, and some village officials were replaced, but essentially it was a case of old wine in new bottles. Most of the changes were semantic. The relationship of the people's council to the NLF administration liberation committee was left deliberately vague, as was its relationship to the Alliance system. In any event the dominant force within the village remained the PRP, working either through the people's council or the NLF committee.

The third cluster was the most important one and the only one fully to survive the test of time. It did so by merging the various other groups into one general matrix that became known as the Alliance of National and Democratic Peace Forces of Vietnam.[11] Initially, the Alliances were urban-based, in Hué, Saigon, Da Nang, Nha Trang, and briefly in Dalat. First public reference to them came in a Hué area radio broadcast on the night of January 31, 1968; *Nhan Dan*, the major newspaper in Hanoi, took note of them on February 2. The Hué Alliance distributed leaflets during the Tet attack, the first week in February, informing the population that it stood for: "(1) the overthrow of the Thieu government; (2) regaining national sovereignty, ending this unjust war and forcing withdrawal of all U.S. and satellite troops; (3) restoration of peace and building of an independent, democratic, peaceful and neutral South Viet-

[11] The Vietnamese name is *Lien Mien Dan Toc Dan Chu va Hoa Binh a Viet Nam.*

nam;[12] and (4) negotiation with the NLF to achieve these objectives."

In the rural areas the Alliance idea, as originally conceived, was a lesser part of the Revolutionary Council arrangement — a sort of village- and district-level negotiational front group. When the seizure of power failed, the leadership was faced with the choice of either quietly disbanding the Alliance system or turning it into new channels. It chose the latter and assigned the Alliance new tasks, both external and internal. The external task was to offer itself to the world as the "third force" in Vietnam, standing somewhere between the NLF-PRP power contenders and those in Saigon. The internal task was to upgrade itself and secure a political foothold; in the cities this, at best, would be tenuous and, of necessity, deeply covert; in the rural areas it involved incorporating the Revolutionary Council idea, not for administrative reasons but in an effort to develop a political base for the Alliance and prevent it from being dismissed by the world simply as another Vietnamese political tendency — with nothing to offer beyond its good offices. Hence, the Alliance increasingly sought to portray itself as an important, authentic, non-Communist, political force in South Vietnam with its own followers, its own programs, and its own political power:

> I hope that you understand the history and the nature of the Alliance. The United States and the Thieu-Ky traitors drove the people to death and devastated the land. In the face of this miserable situation, the intellectuals, the younger generation, the progressive bourgeoisie, and the progressive elements of various political parties and religious groups sought measures to restore peace. These non-Communist nationalists and patriots, who do

[12] The DRV version of this statement, published in *Nhan Dan,* February 2, 1968, omitted the word "neutral."

not belong to the Liberation Front . . . decided to cooperate with the NFLSV in order to achieve peace. The National, Democratic, and Peace Forces in various districts have inaugurated revolutionary committees or revolutionary organs of power to control administrative work in the newly liberated areas. For instance, revolutionary committees were formed in almost all the villages and hamlets in Thua Thien Province during the heroic resistance in Hué for a month by the Liberation forces at the time of the Tet offensive (1968), revolutionary committees were formed in 170 villages in the Delta district. Thus, revolutionary committees are being formed one after another throughout the country under the guidance of the National, Democratic, and Peace Forces.[13]

The result has been that the Alliance has assumed a dual image, or schizoid personality, as an alternative to the NLF or at least as a neutral middleman between the two forces, and as an integral part of an *apparat* that includes the NLF, PRP, and DRV. For example, shortly after its formation the Hué Alliance broadcast this message throughout Central Vietnam:

Compatriots: The revolution we waited and yearned for has broken out. The heroic Saigon people and the revolutionary armed forces are launching attacks against the Independence Palace and other main offices and organizations of the Thieu-Ky puppet regime. A splendid spring is blossoming throughout our country. The aforementioned, resounding victories once again mark the unavoidable collapse of the Americans and puppets who are at the end of their trail. Let our compatriots . . . continuously rise up to smash all the bandits' puppet and wicked organizations, level off all the remaining strategic hamlets, chop to pieces the strategic highways, dismantle all war bases, wreck bridges and incessantly coordinate with the armed forces to stand up with a general uprising spirit. . . . Forward! Victory will be ours![14]

[13] *Tokyo Yomiuri,* a two-part article, July 6 and 7, 1968, based on an interview with an Alliance press spokesman in Paris, by the Yomiuri Paris Bureau.

[14] An "Appeal of the National Leadership Committee of the Alliance

This is hardly the language of a good-offices middleman seeking to negotiate differences between two contending forces. However, when the purpose of the Alliance later became to convince the world that it could mediate between the NLF and, primarily, the Americans (rather than the GVN) and bring peace to Vietnam through coalition government, its tone became more reasonable. Compare the preceding message, of February 1968, with this statement by an Alliance spokesman in July 1968:

> The Alliance consists of South Vietnamese nationalists. Their greatest task is the restoration of peace. The Alliance hopes that Vietnam will become an independent, neutral, prosperous, democratic country. Furthermore, South Vietnam will be a democratic, non-Communist, neutral country, independent of North Vietnam, for the time being after the restoration of peace. . . . The Alliance is completely independent of the Liberation Front. The Alliance calls for democracy, neutrality, and noncommunism. The political platform of the Liberation Front will not force communism on South Vietnam. The Alliance has decided to cooperate with the Liberation Front just because the platform is compatible with the desires of the South Vietnamese people. The alliance will become the sole political medium to create a peaceful political system on the basis of military power of the Liberation Front. Meanwhile, the Liberation Front will aid the Alliance with its military power for the restoration of peace.[15]

The national Alliance (as opposed to the various city Alliances) was formed at a "founding congress" held April 20–21, 1968, at a rubber plantation outside Mimot, Cambodia. A manifesto issued at this time outlined its objectives:

> 1. The South Vietnamese people are very eager for peace, but peace in honor and freedom. The Vietnam Alliance of National,

---

of National and Peace Forces," broadcast by Radio Liberation in Vietnamese, February 2, 1968.

[15] Yomiuri interview, *op. cit.*

Democratic, and Peace Forces advocates winning back South Vietnam's independence and sovereignty and demanding that the U.S. Government end the war, withdraw U.S. and allied troops from South Vietnam, abolish all U.S. military bases, and respect Vietnam's independence and sovereignty, as specified in the 1954 Geneva Agreements on Vietnam. South Vietnam's national independence, sovereignty, and territorial integrity must be recognized and respected by all governments throughout the world. The Vietnam Alliance of National, Democratic, and Peace Forces is ready to discuss these problems with the U.S. Government.

2. The South Vietnam National Liberation Front, a patriotic force, which has greatly contributed to the mobilization, organization, and leadership of the struggle against foreign invasion during past years, cannot be excluded from settlement of all problems in South Vietnam. We advocate contacts with the South Vietnam National Liberation Front to win back national independence, restore peace, reconstruct the country, and establish conditions for our people to lead to a life of happiness in freedom.

3. The political regime in South Vietnam will be a Republic. The people will live in true freedom and democracy. Such rights as freedom of speech, press, religion, movement, congregation, organization, foreign travel, and so forth, will be guaranteed. There will be no difference whatsoever in the treatment of individuals. All organs of state power will be elected by the people through just and honest elections. People of all walks of life, men as well as women, and all nationalities and religions will be represented in those organs of state power. All Vietnamese will be equal in all respects. The rights of our people living abroad will be cared for, and the legitimate rights of foreigners living in Vietnam will be respected. The economy of South Vietnam should be independent and prosperous. Agriculture should be developed, and business, industry, trade, and transportation should be encouraged in order to make the country prosperous. Workers' rights and those of people of all walks of life should be respected. An agrarian reform program should be carried out correctly in South Vietnam to form a basis for agricultural development and improve living conditions and purchasing power of our peasants and contribute to over-all development of the national economy.

When peace is restored, the immediate measures to be taken are to heal war wounds and build and develop the economy. South Vietnam appeals to all countries that are not bound by any political conditions to assist her in terms of capital, technical aid, and specialists. Vietnam will try by all means to get rid of all the bad influence of the degrading culture and foster long-standing national traditions. Activities of social interest and education and examination systems should be fostered. Our compatriots belonging to ethnic minorities living in South Vietnam and old people, children, women, wounded and sick soldiers, and the disabled should be cared for.

4. South Vietnam will be an independent country with full sovereignty, observing the policy of a nonaligned country having relations with all countries regardless of their political systems, provided that those countries actually respect the independence and territorial integrity of Vietnam. South Vietnam has highly respected its friendship with the neighboring Cambodian and Laotian countries.

5. Concerning the problem of national unification: national unification is the earnest aspiration and social duty of all our people. In actuality, there are now two different political regimes in the two zones of our country. The problem of national unification cannot be settled at a moment's notice. Therefore, the two zones must discuss and negotiate between themselves on the basis of equality and respect for each other's characteristics with a view to advancing toward achieving national unification through peaceful means. Pending this unification, there must be relations between the two zones in the fields of economy, culture, correspondence, free movement, and so forth. Southern compatriots, regrouped in the north, will be free to return to the south in accordance with their desires. Conversely, Northern compatriots who went south will be free to return to the north.[16]

Important persons associated with the national Alliance were these:

Trinh Dinh Thao, sixty-eight, is a long-time radical close

[16] Radio Liberation in Vietnamese to South Vietnam, April 25, 1968.

to being eccentric. He was born in North Vietnam, and is a Confucianist. He studied law in France, where he embraced Trotskyism, then returned to practice law in Hanoi and later in Hué and Saigon. He served as Minister of the Interior (that is, Justice) in the 1945 Tran Trong Kim Cabinet during the Japanese occupation. In 1954, 1959, and 1965 he was arrested by the GVN, the first two times for activities connected with "peace movements" (in association with NLF Central Committee Chairman Nguyen Huu Tho, who also was at that time a Saigon lawyer), and the third time during a Buddhist demonstration; but he was released after each arrest. Although he has not actively practiced law in recent years, he has been active in fringe-type left-wing movements, including one that stands for repartition of Vietnam (into the three former divisions of Annam, Tonkin, and Cochin China), with Central Vietnam or Annam becoming a neutral buffer state between the other two, and with Bao Dai returning as Emperor of Annam. His wife is from a well-to-do Southern family; one son is a Saigon lawyer, and a daughter is married to a successful Saigon jeweler. In February 1968 he left Saigon. He is chairman of the Alliance.

Lam Van Tet, in his late fifties, is an old-line Southern maverick radical, having been active most of his life in off-beat dissident political movements. A surveyor (or, according to his description, an engineer) by profession, he made a large amount of money (some sources say he is a millionaire) in land dealings in the Saigon area. A student Trotskyite, he was jailed at least twice by the French. In 1963–1964 he was a member of the largely honorary Council of Notables, set up by the Duong Van Minh government after the overthrow of the Diem regime to act as an official advisory body to the ruling Military Directorate. In 1966 he ran for the Senate, but his slate was defeated. He has religious connections in the Cao Dai and was chairman in 1964 of the All Religions Citizens' Front, composed of representatives of the Cao Dai, Hoa Hao, Buddhists, and Catholics (represented by Reverend Hoang Quynh), which sought ways to make relations among the various religious groups in South Vietnam more amiable. He is vice-chairman of the Alliance.

Thich Don Hau, in his early forties, is a militant Mahayana Buddhist monk from Hué, associated with Hué's prestigious Thien Mu temple (where worships, among others, ex-Emperor Bao Dai's mother). Although closely associated with, and perhaps even the heir apparent at one time to, Vietnam's most famous militant Buddhist, Thich Tri Quang, Don Hau was not a political activist until 1966 when he entered the Buddhist Struggle Movement. His behavior at that time led some Vietnamese to label him a "sleeper" Communist; on the other hand, there was speculation in Hué in early 1968 that he was an involuntary supporter of the Alliance. Radio Liberation throughout 1968 broadcast several statements in his name. He is a Centerite, and has been listed by the Alliance as a vice-chairman.

Ton That Duong Ky, in his mid-thirties, is a history professor of royal blood from Central Vietnam. An active lay Buddhist, his moment of fame came in 1965 when he was arrested with two other persons on charges of "advocating false peace" and marched across the Ben Hai River bridge into North Vietnam, a scene recorded by a battery of television cameras. Hanoi quickly moved him on to Paris, from which he made his way, apparently with GVN knowledge, back to Saigon a year later. Considered highly intelligent although somewhat unstable by persons who knew him while he was teaching at Saigon and Hué

Universities, he has what probably is the most powerful position in the Alliance, that of secretary-general.

Le Van Giap, at sixty-one, is *éminence grise* of the Alliance, a former (and perhaps still) member of the French Deuxième Bureau. Born in North Vietnam, the son of a mandarin, he served French intelligence through the 1940's, switching sides to the Viet Minh in 1950, and switching again (apparently) in 1954 when he moved south to Saigon. He taught at Jean Jacques Rousseau high school in Saigon, where he earned a reputation for being strongly pro-French; he was active in French intellectual and cultural circles in the south. His official position is chairman of the Saigon-Cholon-Gia Dinh branch of the Alliance.

Dr. Duong Quynh Hoa, forty-two, is a French-educated obstetrician believed by Vietnamese police to be a member of the Commuinst Party (the only person in the Alliance leadership so labeled). While studying in France, she became engaged to a French Communist, who died shortly thereafter; she returned to Saigon and set up practice, becoming well-to-do in the process but never marrying. In 1961 she was arrested by the GVN after a Communist defector told the police she was a member of an important Communist cell in Saigon; later she was released for lack of corroborating evidence. Her brother, a lawyer in the mountain town of Dalat, was set upon, robbed, and murdered in the early 1960's, apparently by a gang of thugs, although she told friends later she thought the killing was government-ordered. A Southerner, she is assistant secretary-general of the Alliance.

Le Hieu Dang, in his mid-twenties, is a skilled agit-prop worker active in 1965–1967 in the Saigon Student Union, which he served as deputy chairman and chief of the propaganda department. A militant Buddhist from Central Vietnam, he is considered highly idealistic by former friends who knew him as a law student at Saigon University. He is editor of the Alliance newspaper, *Save Our Land* (*Cuu Lay Que Huong*). His position is assistant secretary-general of the Alliance.

Thanh Nghi, in his mid-thirties, is a Saigon journalist and the son of Hoang Thong, a well-known Southern artist. Well educated by the French, he is the author of a French-Vietnamese dictionary. His writings tended to be pro-NLF and were strongly pro-French.

Others in the Alliance's Central Committee include: (1) *Nguyen Van Kiet,* a French-educated Southerner and a Buddhist from Can Tho, former Saigon University French literature professor, and ex-GVN Ministry of Education official in the field of primary education; (2) *Tran Trieu Luat,* a Southerner and An Quang Buddhist, an ex-student radical who had been vice-chairman of the Saigon Student Union in 1964–1965, editor of the magazine *Student,* and an active member of the university autonomy movement; after graduation from Saigon University in 1967, he accepted a university position as instructor in the education faculty; (3) *Huynh Van Nghi,* a former teacher from the Mekong Delta, active at one time in the Hoa Hao sect.

In the Hué Alliance the most prominent members were: Chairman *Le Van Hao,* former ethnology professor at Hué University, an active lay Buddhist whose family at one time was closely connected with the Ngo Dinh Diem family; Vice-Chairman *Mrs. Tuong Vy,* former principal of the Dong Khanh girls' school in Hué whose two daughters are married to prominent GVN officials; Vice-Chairman *Thich*

Don Hau (described earlier); and Secretary-General *Hoang Phu Ngoc Tuong,* a protégé of Don Hau and an active Buddhist militant from Central Vietnam. *Ho Huu Nhat,* about whom little is known, is listed as secretary-general of the Alliance branch in Saigon.

Certain characteristics of the leadership are worth noting. Virtually all the leaders of the Alliance have close, active identification with religious organizations in Vietnam, and the Alliance clearly is religious-oriented, probably as a tactic for gaining support. In addition, most of the leaders have some ties with the Vietnamese educational establishment. Thus much of the Alliance output is directed at the devoutly religious and at the student-intellectual, with the themes aimed at the former being chiefly war horror and peace at any price, while to the latter the appeals are idealistic, nationalistic, and anti-Establishment. It also appears that a disproportionate number of the leaders have a French education or other unusually close ties with the French. There definitely is a disproportionate number of Centerites in the movement, the ratio of Southerners to Centerites to Northerners being 2:4:1 (compared with the national South Vietnam ratio of 10:5:1). Beyond this, more subjectively, the leadership has an aura about it of lost causes, dilettantism, and amateurism in politics (except for Ton That Duong Ky and Le Van Giap).

The Alliance, through 1968 inside Vietnam, tried to generate a spirit of enthusiastic support for its program; but even among the Vietnamese at whom the movement was primarily directed — the devoutly religious, the disaffected student and intellectual, and the war-weary city dweller — the Alliance was not taken seriously, nor did its appeals have much impact even though the sentiments they expressed are widely held in Vietnam. The GVN did appear to take the Alliance more seriously. On July 21, 1968, the ten members of the Alliance Central Committee were tried *in absentia* on treason charges, found guilty, and sentenced to death, and all of their property was confiscated.

The Alliance maintains an extraordinarily close relationship with the NLF, the PRP, and the DRV, far greater than — in an outsider's view — prudence or judgment would dictate. The DRV, the Soviet Union, and the Communist bloc nations became its most vocal supporters; its public pronouncements were carried exclusively by Radio Liberation in South Vietnam and Radio Hanoi; and its information offices in Paris were in the NLF headquarters. In fact, DRV and NLF representatives around the world spoke publicly and authoritatively on all sorts of internal Alliance matters. All this had the distinct effect of blurring the image of the Alliance as a "third force."

The Alliance as a front for a front might be new, but the technique is old and orthodox in Vietnamese politics. One could almost write the past four decades of Vietnamese history in terms of front mergers. The special genius in this art of organization juggling is Ho Chi Minh. In the 1930's and 1940's he created a series of front organizations, one engulfing the next like the famous cartoon of a line of fish each about to be swallowed by a larger fish swimming behind it. With great skill he created, developed, and then merged a series of united-front organizations, each sizably larger than its predecessor, yet at all times under his control: the Indochinese Communist Party (which itself was a merger by Ho Chi Minh of three Communist parties) was merged with other organizations into the Viet Minh. This was merged with a group of organizations creating the

Lien Viet, which in turn was merged with still other groups into the Fatherland Front. One is left with a sense of *déjà vu* about the Alliance.

The Democratic Republic of Vietnam[17]

Since its creation in 1945 the DRV leadership has relentlessly and undeviatingly pursued one objective: the control and governing of all Vietnam under the Communist banner, or in its parlance, "the liberation and reunification of the Fatherland." Ho Chi Minh pursued this goal long before there was a DRV. A sampling of his thinking on the subject of unification, typical of the DRV leadership:

> Peace has been restored in Indo-China on the basis of recognition of independence, sovereignty, unity and territorial integrity of Viet Nam, Laos and Cambodia; peace has been brought to us by the 1954 Geneva Conference. It cannot be consolidated as long as our country remains partitioned by the provisional demarcation line at the 17th parallel. . . . Thus peace and national reunification are our main demands for the time being.[18]

[17] North Vietnam covers an area of 63,344 square miles and is slightly smaller than South Vietnam. Its 1968 population was estimated at 18,900,000, about 90 per cent of whom live in the Red River Delta and the adjacent coastal plain to the North. Lao Dong Party membership is about 800,000. PAVN, in mid-1968, was composed of about 500,000 men, of whom approximately 100,000 were in South Vietnam and 40,000 in Laos. PAVN had about twelve divisions of 12,000 men each, an organic military infrastructure, a 3,000-man Air Force, and a 2,500-man Navy. In addition, it has an estimated 250,000-man Regional Militia Force divided into five military zones across North Vietnam and a 28,000-man quasi-military Armed Public Security Force. Backing up those regular and regional military forces is a Self-Defense Force, a paramilitary organization of some three million men and women; members of this organization receive military training, perform local security missions, act as production workers where required, and serve as a backup reserve for PAVN.

[18] Speech at the Tenth DRV National Day Anniversary, September 1955. Published in a booklet entitled *For a Lasting Peace, for a People's Democracy* (Hanoi, December 1955).

The North is the foundation, the root of the struggle for complete national liberation and the reunification of the country. That is why everything we are doing in the North is aimed at strengthening both the North and the South. Therefore to work here is the same as struggling in the South; it is to struggle for the South and for the whole of Viet Nam. . . . The North is being increasingly consolidated to become a firm support, a strong base for our entire people's struggle.[19]

The National Assembly has discussed the question of national reunification. . . . To achieve national reunification all our people must unite closely, make further efforts to consolidate the North and make it a basis for national liberation. Our deputies have voiced the iron will of our people in the work of national reunification.[20]

Our Party's immediate task is to lead the people to intensify the emulation to increase production and practice economy to build Socialism in the North in order to serve as a firm base for the struggle for national reunification.[21]

We are resolved to drive away the U.S. aggressors and to defend the freedom, independence and territorial integrity of our Fatherland. . . . The government of the DRV solemnly declares its unswerving stand: to resolutely defend Viet Nam's independence, sovereignty, unity and territorial integrity. Viet Nam is one, the Vietnamese people are one. . . .[22]

We should strive to defend and build North Viet Nam into a stronghold and wholeheartedly assist the liberation of South Viet Nam. . . . Again we say to President Johnson . . . the problem

[19] Letter to South Vietnam cadres regrouped in the North, June 1956. Quoted by Bernard Fall, *Ho Chi Minh on Revolution: Selected Writings, 1920–66* (New York: The New American Library, 1967), pp. 272–273.

[20] Report on the Sixth Session of the National Assembly (First Legislature), February 15, 1957. Quoted in *ibid.*, p. 278.

[21] Speech at ceremonies commemorating the 30th Anniversary of the Founding of the Lao Dong Party, January 5, 1960. Quoted in *ibid.*, p. 308.

[22] Address to the National Assembly, April 1965. *Viet Nam Courier*, April 15, 1965.

of reunification Viet Nam must be settled by the Vietnamese people themselves without foreign interference. . . . Long live a peaceful, reunified, independent, democratic and prosperous Viet Nam.[23]

The objective was within DRV grasp in 1954. The Viet Minh had defeated the French, at least psychologically, and all of Vietnam was theirs for the taking; they had achieved victory, only to be deprived of its fruit by their erstwhile allies; "sold out" perhaps would be not too strong a term. The Soviets, as part of a deal to scuttle the European Defense Community, and the Chinese, then pressing Nehru's *panch shila* (coexistence) and what was soon to be called the "Spirit of Bandung in Asia," convinced Ho Chi Minh and his fellow Politburo members to settle for temporary partition, using the argument that all the country soon would be theirs. This hope was soon dashed.

Nevertheless, the DRV continued to search for a means of unifying Vietnam, and its efforts to date easily can be traced. From about 1954 to about 1958, it sought to achieve unification by relying on French diplomacy, hoping that Paris would be able to implement the Geneva Accords. In 1959 there began a more direct route, which was to encourage through the instrument of the NLF the rise of social pathology or simple anarchy in South Vietnam, hoping that out of the chaos there would come into power in Saigon a government agreeable to the idea of unification. A great deal of anarchy was thus created, but the DRV did not achieve its objective. Then in 1964 there began a third effort, a direct military one: the dispatch of PAVN soldiers into South Vietnam with orders to achieve unification by pure military force. None of these three means — diplomacy,

[23] A Speech to the National Assembly, April 1966. *Viet Nam Courier,* April 28, 1966.

proxy struggle, or direct military—is mutually exclusive. Abandonment of any one may be temporary. The effort does suggest a high level of rationality in DRV thinking and indicates, if nothing else, that the leadership has no hesitation about abandoning one method or policy when another appears more promising.

Communist China

Communist China has had an active interest in the Vietnam war since its inception and since 1965, at least, has been an important participant in the war. As of late 1968 some 80,000 to 100,000 People's Liberation Army (PLA) troops were on duty in North Vietnam.[24] Many of them were noncombatant, such as railway battalions, warehouse and petroleum depot troops; but some were combatant, for example, antiaircraft crews. Because North Vietnam has no full-scale armament factories (as opposed to assembly plants), all of its weapons and ammunition must be imported. The bulk comes from China. Estimates on the amount and value of this military hardware, admittedly difficult to determine, ranged in 1968 from a conservative low of U.S. $250 million per month to three times this rate. By all estimates the Chinese contribution is at least double that of the Soviet Union. Other economic relations also are close: from 12 to 15 per cent of the rice eaten in North Vietnam comes from China along with an estimated 25 per cent of the consumer goods.

The Chinese engage in a great deal of sideline cheering

[24] However, in late 1968 there were persistent reports out of North Vietnam that the Chinese were reducing their troop strength in North Vietnam. Probably the level of support, although increasing or decreasing according to need, will continue at an adequate level unless Hanoi turns, in Chinese eyes, in the direction of revisionism.

but indicate considerable reluctance to go beyond a training and quartermaster role. If one judges by official Peking pronouncements over the past three years, the Chinese leadership believes that the DRV and the NLF are fighting the war in the wrong way, in fact, are doing virtually everything wrong.[25] China would like to see North Vietnam and the NLF pursue a protracted conflict as self-sufficiently as possible, bleeding and humiliating America but giving it no excuse for striking harder at North Vietnam or at China. It would also like to see revolutionary fervor if not turmoil in Asia maintained and *détente* between the United States and the Soviet Union prevented or hampered. Most Sinologists whom the author knows — not only American but Chinese, British, Japanese, and Vietnamese — seem agreed that China will not dispatch PLA troops into South Vietnam unless its leaders perceive a direct threat to China, which is not the case under American rules of engagement as of late 1968. The chief significance of Communist victory in Vietnam to the Chinese — beyond the mystic benefits of proving the power of a people's war — would be a diminution of U.S. military prowess in Asia. But the full meaning of Vietnam to China goes beyond ordinary twentieth-century foreign policies. The Chinese world view contains the conviction that China has an *inherent right* to monitor the destinies of the peoples on its perimeter, those around the Middle Kingdom, and that these peoples have an *obligation* to defer to China, never to make a major governmental move, for example, without first clearing it with Peking.

[25] For example, if one reads the famed Lin Piao article "Long Live the People's War" (September 1965) as if one were an NLF cadre, what Lin seems to be saying is that *everything* the NLF does violates "people's war" principles. See *Jen-minh Jih pao,* September 2, 1965; also see William E. Griffith, *Sino-Soviet Relations, 1964–1965* (Cambridge, Mass.: The M.I.T. Press, 1967), Document 30.

This attitude of suzerainty—actually not so much an attitude as a highly ethnocentric unquestioned assumption—is far older than communism in China, virtually as old as China itself. But in this age of ultranationalism, in which each subgroup of human beings around the world is supremely conscious of its own identity and separateness, such a demand amounts to disassociation from reality, something that bothers the Chinese not a whit. This Chinese view of Vietnam will last far beyond the present war.

For its part, the NLF regards China as a big brother, older, wiser, stronger and a source of great support. A clandestine NLF newspaper published in the Mekong Delta in late 1966 declared:

> We strive to learn from the Chinese People's Liberation Army about a transcendental, valiant, fighting spirit; about advanced techniques and strategy; about the art of people's war; and about the patterns of building internal ranks. We are determined to apply creatively their valuable experiences . . . in our anti-U.S. national salvation struggle. The South Vietnamese people constantly receive great, sincere, generous, steady, and efficient support and aid from the Communist Party, the government, and the people of fraternal China. . . . In addition to their full support in the political and moral fields, the fraternal Chinese people have constantly supported and helped the South Vietnamese people in an efficient and many-sided way in the material field. . . . The Southern Liberation Armed Forces are determined . . . not to allow the United States to use South Vietnam as a springboard for launching crimes against the Chinese people. This is our sacred obligation toward . . . the brother Chinese People's Republic.

A propaganda leaflet widely distributed in the South declared:

> Workers everywhere in China have doubled and tripled their factory output to help Vietnam under the slogan: Every meter of cloth produced is a meter of skin taken from an American,

> and every yard of cotton is a yard of American nerve fiber. . . . Thus the 650 million Chinese have demonstrated their sincere friendship for Vietnam [and] are bound together [with its people] under the hammer and sickle flag of International Communism. . . .

The relationship of the Chinese Communists to the Vietnam war is a highly dynamic one, always in tension and steadily in flux. The fact of the war is never as important to the Chinese leaders as are those internal events in China collectively described by that vague term "Cultural Revolution," which is here defined as the political, ideological, and personal struggle between the ideologues (or Maoists) and the pragmatists (whose nominal symbol is Liu Shao-ch'i but whose real strength is the generals of the People's Liberation Army). Neither is the war in Vietnam as important to the Chinese leaders as are the maneuvers and battles in the Sino-Soviet struggle, and in those instances where the leadership has been forced to choose between serving the struggle against the Russians and serving the Vietnamese, the former purpose unfailingly has prevailed. Thus any full analysis of China and the Vietnam war would require discussion both of internal events in China and of the Sino-Soviet dispute. Such, obviously, is beyond the scope of this book. The hopes of China, as opposed to her specific goals, seem reasonably clear: diminution of American military prowess in areas adjacent to China, preferably under humiliating circumstances; reaffirmation of China's moral and spiritual dominion over rimland barbarian countries; and assumption by governments in such countries of a deferential posture toward Peking in all major matters. The finite goals of China are much less easily discerned. It appears to be the consensus of the China watchers and other Sinologists whom the author consults that, in oversimplified terms, this is the situation: In the struggle between the ideologues and the pragmatists, eventually the pragmatists will win, must win.[26] This is not to say that Mao Tse-tung himself necessarily will lose but that the policies within the Cultural Revolution for which he stood — bypassing the Party apparatus to establish a new power base called the Red Guard or the establishment of the "constant revolution" (life at the bottom of a malted milk mixer, as one Hong Kong Chinese put it) — will not endure and will gradually be relegated to history's dustbin. The pragmatists and the ideologues differ sharply in their view of the Vietnam war. The pragmatists ask themselves what exactly is there in the war for China, and the answer for the most part is negative. The ideologues, on the other hand, don't even ask the question. They *know* that the war has great meaning, mystical and indefinable perhaps, but nevertheless real. The support it generates will continue, unless, of course, Hanoi turns "revisionist." Thus, if this assessment is correct, that ultimately at least the pragmatists will win in the struggle with the ideologues and when victorious, because of their very nature, will diminish rather than increase Chinese involvement in the Vietnam war, then obviously the Chinese role in Vietnam counts for less and less. Of course, there are too many variables to make this idea more than a useful hypothesis in evaluating news from China.

The Soviet Union

The Soviet Union's influence in Vietnam has varied considerably over the years. It was relatively strong in 1960 to

[26] In fact, they have won, according to some China watchers. See Robert Elegant, "China's Next Phase," *Foreign Affairs,* Vol. 46, No. 1 (October 1967), pp. 137–150.

mid-1963, then dropped off sharply until early 1965 when the DRV found itself desperately in need of certain sophisticated weapons such as MIG fighter planes and surface-to-air missiles. Accordingly, the Soviet Union's stock rose since it was the only source of supply. At all times, however, the Soviet influence has been considerably less than that of the Chinese, although neither has been excessive. Ironically, the North Vietnamese are offered a great deal of military assistance along with a quantity of advice by both the Russians and the Chinese, and because of the Sino-Soviet dispute, they can take the aid from both and the advice from neither. Thus neither side has much leverage.

The Soviet Union's chief and overriding interest in the Vietnam war appears to be a negative one, ensuring that the conflict does not get out of hand and turn into a nuclear war, which inevitably would involve the Soviet Union. Some Kremlinologists, especially in Europe, argue that the Soviet Union genuinely wants peace in Vietnam, as a means of achieving *détente* with the United States. From the vantage point of Saigon, however, there is little to support this contention. It is true the Soviet Union has exhibited some restraint in opening her weapons warehouses to the North Vietnamese — it has not given antiship missiles to the North Vietnamese which it has given to Nasser — but this perhaps is mere prudence.

The Republic of Vietnam

What the South Vietnamese want, quite obviously, is peace — though not at any price. Most Vietnamese feel they have fought too long and sacrificed too much simply to purchase the peace of a grave. Equally obviously, Vietnamese want national development or modernization or nation building or whatever term one chooses to describe the expectation of the good life by ex-colonial peoples. In both dreams the people of South Vietnam consistently have been frustrated. During the Viet Minh war a certain amount of national development went on in Tonkin, under the Viet Minh. In Annam, under Emperor Bao Dai (and the French ruling in his name), there was less progress. In Cochin China, a virtual colony of France, there was no progress at all. South Vietnam, under President Diem, saw a certain amount of national development: economic rationalization, governmental reorganization, creation of a national army. But Diem, more traditional than reactionary, was only mildly interested in many of the nation-building activities (he was not particularly concerned about building basic industries, for example, preferring to keep Vietnam agrarian), and in any case the effort was interrupted by the resumption of war. But since 1966, in spite of the war and in some ways because of it, a surprising amount of nation-building activity has gotten underway. Economists in Vietnam believe that within a year or two after the end of hostilities Vietnam will be at the point of economic take-off.

South Vietnamese take an elemental view of the struggle and the objectives of their government: they want withdrawal into North Vietnam of PAVN troops now in the South, along with the Northern elements in the NLF civilian structure; they want, as the only workable way to peace, integration of the NLF members back into the society, but obviously not under circumstances in which the latter dominate (after all, that is what the war is all about to the South Vietnamese).

Foreign Minister Tran Van Do's statement on the conditions for peace in Vietnam represents both in substance and flavor the South Vietnamese attitude toward the struggle:

1. Since the war now in progress in Vietnam was provoked by Communist aggression and subversion, it is essential, first of all, that these subversive and military activities undertaken, directed, and supported from abroad against the independence and freedom of the people of South Vietnam cease, and that the principle of noninterference in the internal affairs of the two zones, a principle that was laid down in the 1954 Geneva agreement and in international law, be respected. Consequently, the Communist regime of Hanoi must dissolve all these front organizations and agencies it has created in South Vietnam under the title the Front for the Liberation of the South, Liberation Radio Station, and People's Revolutionary Party, and it must remove from South Vietnam the troops and the political and military leaders it has sent there illegally.

2. The internal affairs of the South Vietnamese people must be left to the discretion of those people in conformity with democratic principles and without any foreign interference from whatever source. That will be feasible, obviously, only when the aggression by the Communist regime of Hanoi and its campaign of intimidation to which the people of South Vietnam have been subjected have been terminated.

3. As soon as aggression has ceased, the Government of the Republic of Vietnam and the nations that come to its aid will be able to suspend the military measures in the territory of South Vietnam and beyond its boundaries that are now necessary to defend that territory against Communist aggression. Moreover, the Government of the Republic of Vietnam is prepared to ask friendly nations then to remove their military forces from South Vietnam. It reserves the right, however, to take whatever measures are necessary to see that law and order are respected throughout the territory of South Vietnam and to insure the safety of the South Vietnamese people, as well as the right to appeal again for foreign assistance in the case of further aggression or threat of aggression.

4. Lastly, the independence and freedom of the people of South Vietnam must be effectively guaranteed.[27]

The United States and Other Pacific Nations

The United States, as of late 1968, had about 550,000 troops in South Vietnam, of whom about 15 per cent were combatant (45 per cent were engaged in what is called combat support — that is, directly supporting the fighting man — and 40 per cent were what was called administrative support). Other Pacific Ocean powers with troops in Vietnam were: the Republic of Korea, Kingdom of Thailand, Republic of the Philippines, Australia, and New Zealand, for a total troop strength of about 90,000 men.[28]

Listing the objectives of the United States in Vietnam presents a major problem in distinguishing that which is paramount, immediate, and directly germane to Vietnam and that which is primarily relevant to the domestic U.S. scene. The approach here, perhaps somewhat parochial, attempts to confine itself to the meaning of Vietnam to the United States in Vietnam only, and not to the meaning of Vietnam to the United States at home.

American objectives in Vietnam vary in degree of abstraction. Moving along the scale from the concrete to the abstract, America's objectives appear to this author as follows:

1. Withdrawal of U.S. forces from South Vietnam under

27 Tran Van Do, "Conditions for a Just and Lasting Peace" (June 22, 1965) in Wesley R. Fishel, ed., *Vietnam: Anatomy of a Conflict* (Itasca, Ill.: Peacock Press, 1968).

28 As of August 1968, 43 nations (excluding the United States) had given a total of U.S. $80.7 million to South Vietnam in the form of equipment, supplies, expert assistance, and training grants. West Germany (U.S. $21 million since 1954) was the largest. U.S. AID Press Release, Saigon, August 9, 1968.

the circumstances described in the Manila Communiqué, which stated:

(5) Removal of allied military forces.—The people of South Vietnam will ask their allies to remove their forces and evacuate their installations as the military and subversive forces of North Vietnam are withdrawn, infiltration ceases and the level of violence thus subsides.[29]

The most finite objective, therefore, is to get the PAVN infantry divisions back into North Vietnam, along with the Northern civilian elements in the NLF.

2. Removal of all foreign forces from Laos and reinstallation to full effectiveness of the Geneva Agreement of 1962 on Laos. Laos has great relevancy for Vietnam. Many of the more astute observers of the Southeast Asia scene have long insisted that any settlement of the Vietnam war must also involve a settlement in Laos, that stability is not possible in either place unless it exists in both. As of late 1968, at least 40,000 PAVN troops were in Laos and the DRV–Pathet Lao *apparat* controlled about half the country. The Pathet Lao organization is permeated with DRV "advisers," both military and civilian; and they, rather than the Laotian Communist cadres, make the decisions, initiate actions, define doctrine, and in general keep the movement on the track and moving. A haunting specter in Southeast Asia is that of war finally ending in Vietnam only to begin in Laos. At any rate, it seems clear that a settlement of the Vietnam conflict must also involve the matter of DRV activities in Laos.

3. Reaffirmation and reapplication of the principle that there ought not to be any change on the international scene—that is, between countries—*by force*. The United States is

[29] Manila Summit Conference Communiqué issued in Manila, October 25, 1966.

not against unification of Vietnam per se, but it is against unification by force. This is part of a broader American foreign policy principle — the result of the trauma of the 1930's in Europe and later World War II — that those who would change the international scene by force should be stopped early because they never will desist and eventually will have to be stopped at a higher cost. This is seen by America not as a desire to become an international policeman but simply as a matter of national interest. From the American viewpoint, the question of Vietnamese unification should be decided by the people of North Vietnam and the people of South Vietnam in free-choice circumstances.

> [We] deplore the partition of Vietnam into North and South. But this partition brought about by the Geneva Agreements of 1954, however unfortunate and regrettable, will be respected until, by the free choice of all Vietnamese, reunification is achieved.[30]

4. Development of a condition in South Vietnam in which the people can exercise their right of self-determination, to decide without coercion their own political future:

> We [conferees] are united in our determination that the South Vietnamese people shall not be conquered by aggressive forces and shall enjoy the inherent right to choose their own way of life and their own form of government. . . . Our common commitment is to the defense of the South Vietnamese people. Our sole demand on the leaders of North Vietnam is that they abandon their aggression. . . . The people of South Vietnam seek to resolve their own internal differences and to this end are prepared to engage in a program of national reconciliation. When the aggression has stopped, the people of South Vietnam will move more rapidly toward reconciliation of all elements in the society and will move forward, through the democratic process, toward human dignity, prosperity and lasting peace.[31]

[30] *Ibid.*
[31] *Ibid.*

This is the so-called moral obligation, an expression of American moral responsibility for the people of South Vietnam.

5. Maintenance of a credible American commitment, the honoring of treaties, legal obligations, and official understandings. This is not the same as maintenance of American "prestige" in Asia, which in itself is not worth the life of one American. But it does involve picking up the Communist gauntlet of challenge of endurance, for Vietnam above all is a test of wills.

6. Maintenance of an ideological equilibrium in the Pacific. This objective largely accounts for the presence of the various Allied troops in Vietnam. Further, it is a goal probably sought by almost all nations of Asia. Each nation, even the smaller Communist ones, sees as its national interest that no one nation—not China, not Japan, not the United States, not any country—should ever dominate the area. But instead there should be a system in equilibrium. Each also seeks a balance of power in military and economic terms, but ideology is the cutting edge. Concomitant with this, each Asian nation seeks to redress the situation when the balance is threatened. As a Pacific Ocean power, it is in the U.S. interest to contribute toward maintaining this ideological equilibrium; that was the meaning of U.S. involvement in the Korean War, and U.S. leaders see the involvement in Vietnam partly in these terms. It is the chief reason why the allied nations in the Pacific have sent troops to Vietnam:

> The nations represented at this conference are united in . . . their resolve for peace and in their deep concern for the future of Asia and the Pacific. Some of us are now close to the actual danger, while others have learned to know its significance through bitter past experience. . . . At the same time our united purpose

is peace—peace in South Vietnam and in the rest of Asia and the Pacific. . . . We are united in looking to a peaceful and prosperous future for all of Asia and the Pacific.[32]

[32] *Ibid.*

CHAPTER TWO

POLITICS AND SOCIETY

Having briefly considered the contenders and their objectives with respect to war and peace in Vietnam, we now turn to the context in which these forces find themselves. Four aspects of the Vietnamese sociopolitical scene are singled out for consideration as being of primary importance: lingering traditionalism; the various forces that contribute to political and social division, especially geographic regionalism; organizational malaise or weaknesses, especially in the government, stemming partly from Vietnam's heritage and partly from wartime social pathology; and the special problem of legitimatizing distribution of political power and the meaning this has for the future of democracy in Vietnam.

Lingering Traditionalism

The ascriptive forces of traditionalism are strong in Vietnam — deceptively so. As one wise Vietnamese friend observed, "Scratch any Vienamese, and beneath you'll find a true traditionalist." Transitional and modern Vietnamese, perhaps 15 per cent of the total population, are found chiefly in the cities and towns. The 2,561 villages of the country, where live two thirds of the people, are the bastions of traditionalism. Here, as in other traditional societies, people are bound by a tyranny of custom, by an overriding spirit of noninnovation, by a blind acceptance and even defense of hierarchy; and, above all, people tend to see the world as a place over which they have no control. This last aspect distinguishes a traditional from a transitional or modern person. A traditional Vietnamese villager does not understand that he can manipulate the universe, can make things happen or not happen. He does not see himself as a force in the world. He is, of course, but he does not realize it. His view of man and society is much like his view of the most important of all matters to him, the weather. He asks himself: Will the rains come on time, and if they don't, what shall I do? Of course, he has an opinion on the subject—he wants the rains to come on time. But chiefly he thinks in terms of what to do if they don't. Likewise, he looks on the war and Vietnamese politics, not asking who is right and who is wrong—of course, he has opinions on the subject—but wondering what is going to happen and how he should best adjust his behavior accordingly. Life without change—that has been the character of Vietnamese village life. For centuries it has been this way, life flowing on, year after year, with virtually unchanged political concepts, each generation behaving like the one before it. The society was agrarian and homogeneous. The state did not assume much of what has come to be called the socialization process, educating and bringing the young into society as trained, useful members. This was left to the family, and it made family-state relations highly compatible. Demands by the royal court in Hué were low: taxes were to be paid, group labor supplied for road building and other public works, and young men furnished in time of war or invasion. But that was about all, and the villagers lived out their lives without much governmental interference. The village political world was self-contained, with little upward movement. It is true that the mandarin system provided a certain amount of political mobility, based on ability. A youth could enter the world of court politics, but entry was based on written examinations that could be passed only if he schooled himself for years in the Confucian classics. Obviously, this system meant that only a few could be chosen. Concepts of the system, although not the system itself, were preserved by the French colonialists in those few cases in which they did not reserve the prerogatives of government for themselves.

Present-day manifestations of traditionalism are many. Villagers display little interest in national affairs, and because of infrequent dialogue between the leaders and the led, there is weak national consensus as to basic sociopolitical goals, where the society should go and how it ought to get there. Outside the confines of his own village the villager sees a world totally beyond his control. Thus two political arenas exist, one in the village and one in the capital (that is, Saigon and Hué) — two virtually independent political processes, divergent in interest and action, separated by space and time. The result is to block the rise of egalitarianism, impede the development of a single national theater in which the drama of politics can be acted out, retard political mobilization, perpetuate sacred-based politics especially by the Buddhists in Central Vietnam, the heartland of Vietnamese traditionalism, and militate against mass political participation.[1]

The walls are beginning to crumble as traditionalism withers. The most deadly assault on it, of course, is time.

[1] The meaning of the last-mentioned effect, discouraging of political participation, is discussed in the last section of this chapter.

The most effective attacker is the young (Vietnam is a young nation; half the population is eighteen years of age or under). The next generation in Vietnam will be better educated, more familiar with new ideas, less bound by tradition. It will help close the gap between the village and the city and aid greatly in bringing Vietnam into the twentieth century. The war itself helps batter down the village walls. Great numbers of Vietnamese have migrated from their villages to other places. Perhaps one quarter of the South Vietnamese have moved their place of residence since 1960. The refugee — or self-displaced war victim — flees to the city to escape death or the NLF tax collector. About 1.5 million villagers have been registered on GVN refugee relief rolls. An additional estimated million are the so-called hidden refugees, middle-class persons who leave the village to resettle in the cities, but with enough money to support themselves while finding new jobs and thus never appear on relief rolls. Other villagers, especially in Central Vietnam — the only place in the country where one experiences the grinding poverty found in countries like India — move seeking greater economic opportunity. For example, thousands have streamed into Cam Ranh, a sleepy fishing village being transformed into a billion-dollar port, one of the finest in Asia. The number of people living in villages thus dwindles; about 4.2 million now live in greater Saigon-Cholon area, representing 22 per cent of the total population; another 35 per cent live in the district and provincial capitals and other towns with more than 20,000 persons.

Divisiveness

Vietnam is a badly divided society, a fact that tends to be obscured by the admittedly impressive manner in which the Vietnamese have maintained their ethnolinguistic identity over several millennia and in the face of continual efforts by the Chinese to Sinoize if not assimilate them. This pluralism takes many forms. By all odds the most serious is geographic regionalism, a phenomenon not unique to Vietnam, of course, being found in most large countries; but whereas most regionalism is dual — north versus south — in Vietnam the division is threefold: North, Center, and South. It stems from various historical and geographic influences. Vietnam has undergone political division frequently during the past several centuries. In the 1600's it was divided into halves. During the reign of the Tay Son brothers (1788–1802) it was divided into thirds. In 1802 it was united by Emperor Gia Long, only to be divided again into thirds by the French. It became divided into halves as the result of the 1954 Geneva Conference. In part, regionalism results from the Long March to the South, something akin to the American westward or frontier movement. Beginning in the tenth century A.D., Vietnamese began pushing out from the Red River Delta in a movement that continued steadily over an 800-year period and ultimately covered a distance of some 1,500 miles. En route the Vietnamese destroyed the already decadent Cham empire and were in the process of disassembling the Khmer empire, what is present-day Cambodia. As was the case in the American frontier movement, this migration produced a type of individual somewhat different in mental makeup from the Vietnamese left behind, first in the Red River Delta area of the north and later in the imperial court area around Hué. He was a pioneer soul, adventurous, risk-taking, and hardy, differing sharply from his sophisticated cousin who stayed behind in Hanoi and his tradition-minded cousin who remained in

Hué. The seeds of regionalism were planted. Present-day Vietnamese are highly conscious of this triadic divisiveness:

Tonkin, or Tongking, meaning "Eastern Capital" (from the Chinese), is the northern part of the country centered on Hanoi. Under the French it was administered as a direct protectorate with a French *résident supérieur* acting as the viceroy or official representative of the Vietnamese emperor in Hué. Vietnamese now refer to it informally as the North.

Annam, meaning "Pacified South" (in Chinese, it was also the term commonly used by the Chinese for all of Vietnam), was centered around Hué, which under the French was a kingdom, ruled by an emperor, although, of course, actual power resided with the French. Roughly, Central Vietnam is the area running from Thanh Hoa (which is now North Vietnam) southward to Phan Rang (deep in South Vietnam), although it should be kept in mind that there are no sharp dividing lines, this regionalism being as much a state of mind as a geographic fact. This now is referred to generally in Vietnam as the Center.

Cochin China, centered on Saigon, is believed to be a term corrupted from Ke Chiem, the name of the Nguyen dynasty suzerain in Quang Nam province during the seventeenth century. Cochin China was a French possession and not under even nominal control of the emperor. Thus there was not even a façade of native rule in the southern areas. This is now known in Vietnamese parlance as the South.

There developed in Vietnam, as in other countries with a regional division, a host of stereotypes, self-images, and prejudices about the peoples of the three regions. Regionalism now is a force as important as caste is in India. However, it is less intrusive, for unlike the Indian, who must ask a fellow Indian his caste and cannot determine it by looking at him or speaking to him, in Vietnam region is instantly detected by dialect, even by a foreigner with a rudimentary knowledge of the language.[2] Among the characteristics of this regionalism are these:

The Northerner. He sees himself as modern, progressive, scientific-minded, rational, and efficient. He sees the Southerner as lazy, dirty, lethargic, perhaps even dull-witted. The Centerite is considered snobbish, tradition-bound, overly concerned with a remote and largely unimportant past.

The Centerite. He sees himself as the only truly cultured person in Vietnam, the inheritor and protector of a great intellectual and aesthetic tradition, which Northerners and Southerners are able neither to understand nor to appreciate. He regards the Northerner as grasping, money-hungry, and overly sharp in business deals. The Southerner he sees as rustic, boorish, unintellectual.

The Southerner. He regards himself as pacifistic, in harmony with nature in a pastoral sense. Southerners appreciate nature and like to commune with it, thinking nothing of spending a Sunday afternoon meditating on a hillside, a pastime that strikes the Northerner as a waste of time and the Centerite as faintly ridiculous. He strongly regards the Northerner as hot-tempered, aggressive, and warlike. It is not uncommon to encounter in Saigon a Southerner who tells you the Viet Minh was an unnecessary war, that it was started and pursued by hotheaded Northerners, who if they only had had the patience of the Southerners, would have seen the French leave Indochina as the British left India. The Centerite is regarded as a person preoccupied

[2] For example, the word for "yes" in Vietnamese, *da,* is pronounced *zah* in the North, *zha* in the Center, and *yah* in the South.

with political intrigue, often for its own sake, circuitous and ambiguous in speech and deed.

As noted before, the Southerner to Centerite to Northerner ratio in South Vietnam is 10:5:1. Regionalism exists in North Vietnam but is less of a problem because of northern dominance; the ratio there is about 1:3:17.[3] *Hoi chanh,* defectors and returnees, report that geographic divisiveness plagues the NLF leaders; agit-prop cadres lecture to the NLF members constantly on the need to eliminate this sense of regional identification, which they term "bourgeois sentimentality." *Hoi chanh* also report that friction and abrasiveness characterize the relations in PLAF Main Force units commanded by DRV officers and in PAVN units in which Southerners are used as "filler" replacements. Much of what they report is traceable to geographic regionalism. Peoples of these three areas do not work well together, particularly when under strain or pressure.

Minority groups represent another divisive force in Vietnam. Ethnic minorities total about 15 per cent of the population, made up chiefly of the montagnards,[4] ethnic Cambodians (or Khmers), and overseas Chinese, mostly Cantonese.

The montagnards present a bewildering mixture of racial and linguistic groups and subgroups in varying states of civilization. They number about one million and are found almost entirely in the highlands or mountain area of Southern Vietnam. They are not held in high regard by the Vietnamese, and the history of the two groups largely is

[3] Actually there are probably less than 200,000 Cochin Chinese in North Vietnam.

[4] A French word, meaning mountain people, now widely used by foreigners in Vietnam to describe the people of the highlands; it is not an ethnic description but a generic term to cover the whole complex of primitive non-Vietnamese hill peoples.

one of mutual distrust and exploitation by the Vietnamese. Political consciousness is developing among montagnard leaders. There has sprung up a separatist organization called FULRO,[5] which stands for autonomy for montagnards in a vague way, although its exact aims are not clear. Existence of the group does indicate what was long known, that the montagnard leaders are dissatisfied with their status in Vietnam.

Ethnic Cambodians, found chiefly in the Mekong Delta, total perhaps a half-million persons, with another half million carrying some Cambodian blood, the product of Vietnamese-Cambodian marriages. A low level of animosity exists between the Cambodians and Vietnamese, and in general the two groups live together in peace. As most are villagers, their dissatisfaction will grow with the dwindling of traditionalism.

Overseas Chinese in Vietnam number about 1.3 million and are concentrated in Cholon. As elsewhere in Asia, they mostly are merchants and traders. The Chinese at various times in recent years have been subjected to economic discrimination by the Vietnamese. Their condition tends to fluctuate, although it has never become as discriminatory as in Indonesia or the Philippines.

Communication is a strong force for unity, consensus, and political development; thus the lack of a workable communication system in Vietnam is a major divisive force. What makes the communication function so vital is that it fixes political relationships, particularly between the elites and the masses, and thus shapes the subsequent partisanship that develops. What we are concerned with here is far more than mere flow or exchange of ideas. Communica-

[5] Front Unifié de Lutte des Races Opprimées (i.e., United Fighting Front for the Oppressed Races). It first appeared in September 1964.

tion not only bridges the gap between the city people and the villager but also breaks down the village mentality that delays consensus. It is one of the most powerful devices to forge unity. In pre-French Vietnam, outside the village there was little public communication. Life was parochial, elementary, and people were ignorant of the world. Communication within the village was person-to-person. From the outside world there came but a few rumors, perhaps some gossip about the Emperor's court. Both under the Emperor and under the French, the goal of the rulers was, in effect, to prevent consensus and keep the country fragmented. The rulers had a vested interest in divisiveness, and they sat on the crosslines of the channels of communication. Peasant revolts often started when villagers began communicating with nearby villagers.

The strongest present-day force in Vietnam working against the unity that communication helps to bring is the NLF. It expends vast amounts of effort and resources to block communication: NLF-controlled villagers are forbidden to listen to the radio, or even to own radios; only one or two copies of Saigon newspapers are permitted to enter NLF-controlled villages. Special teams of youths in such villages pick up and burn unread GVN leaflets dropped on them from planes.

Religion is still another force that divides Vietnam, although this results more from the fact that politics has not been secularized than from theology. The vast majority of the Vietnamese are at least nominal Buddhists, and Buddhism is perhaps the least dogmatic of the world's major religions, the least demanding in articles of faith. There has been little religious fanaticism in Vietnamese history and the record for the most part is one of great tolerance for varying religions. Unlike Hindus, Vietnamese are not fervently religious people preoccupied with a spiritual quest. Their social system, like that of the Chinese, rests not on revealed religion but on ethics. Religious differences stem rather from political acts, and such has been the case throughout Vietnamese history. In pre-French days Buddhism suffered recurrently at the hands of the Hué court, which tried to encourage Confucianism. Buddhism as a result tended to become militant as well as semicovert, although in the villages it was a case of unobtrusive practice of Buddhism rather than of underground Buddhism. The French also tried to suppress Buddhism, forcing it further toward militancy and clandestinism.

But the great division among Vietnamese Buddhists today is over the proper role of the Buddhist, as a Buddhist, in the affairs of state and the present existence. The genesis of modern-day political activism by Vietnamese Buddhists dates back to the ferment of Asian Buddhism in the 1930's. In that great doctrinal dispute, the orthodox belief in the transience and hence unimportance of life in this world was then challenged by a rising social consciousness with its attendant demand that more attention be paid to life here and now, as, for example, in the development of social welfare activities. This split between the religionist and the activist remains the major division in Vietnamese Buddhism. Politically the Buddhists are split into at least five camps: two are militant Buddhists (a sort of left and right wing); three are the so-called "quiescent" Buddhists who agree that Buddhists ought not to be in politics as Buddhists but disagree on what constitutes politics.

Catholics number about 1.7 million, the majority of whom also are Northerners. They are perhaps the politically best-organized group in the country. The Cao Dai with one million members (5.3 per cent of total population) and the Hoa Hao with 1.55 million (8 per cent of total population), both esoteric religious sects, represent still another dimension to religious divisiveness in Vietnam. Present indications point to a pattern in Vietnam politics in which one of the many political crosscurrents will be religious in nature, that is, Buddhist versus Catholic (as well as Buddhist versus Buddhist). But also it appears likely that the trend will continue to be in the direction of the secularized state.

Still another division is between the military and the civilian. In wartime especially there is a clash between the needs of the soldier turned governmental administrator and the politician-civilian seeking to remain operative in the political arena. Even in wartime there cannot be a political void. A struggle inevitably will go on in Vietnam — as in any country at war — between the military and the civilian. Ngo Dinh Diem was, above all else, a civilian. He distrusted and perhaps disliked the military as a class. But it was Diem who brought the military into civilian governmental administration. He appointed colonels as province chiefs and majors as district chiefs, doing so because he had no choice. He had to get his administrators from somewhere, and the only source beyond the *duc phu su* (that is, the professional government bureaucrat or *fonctionnaire*) or the Northern refugees who had administrative skill and training was the military. As long as the war continues and perhaps long afterward, the soldier will remain a key figure in Vietnamese governmental administration, and the armed forces will remain the largest manpower pool from which to recruit government personnel. (The reference here chiefly is to administrators at the provincial and district levels). Vietnam simply does not have the luxury of choice in being able to decide whether a soldier or civilian shall fill a certain government post. Both will be used. The military can bring much to the system: status, spirit, and solidarity. The military understand modernization and can get things done. Using the military to perform civilian tasks is of course not the same as military control of the government. In the case of Vietnam it is difficult to draw a distinction between military and civilian. There is comfort in the fact that the trend in Vietnam is away from the military junta, that civilians are in the ascendancy, and that the process of "civilianizing" the government is being aided rather than opposed by the military. Although some Vietnamese consider this ironic, the military Vietnamese were actually most responsible for the present trend toward civilian control. It was the Military Directorate that ordered the 1966 Constituent Assembly elections which brought 123 persons to Saigon to write the new constitutions; it was the Directorate that pressed the 123 to get on with the job; and it was the Directorate that took the finished document in the spring of 1967 and implemented it.

The NLF itself, of course, represents a divisive political force in the society, as does the Alliance. The NLF can be thought of as a somewhat disloyal opposition that divides the people of the South, often on a geographic basis; the NLF is strongest, because of family ties, in the Central Vietnamese provinces of Binh Dinh, Phu Yen, and Quang Ngai.

Finally there are the more or less ubiquitous forces that divide, which should not be overemphasized with respect to Vietnam: the rich versus the poor; the young versus those over thirty; the conservatives versus the liberals; the advocates of change versus the advocates of the status quo; the intellectuals versus everyone else. They simply add their weight to the already badly gyrating teeter-totter.

Organizational Malaise

Not only is Vietnam a badly divided society; it is a badly organized one. Its many organizational problems—social as well as political—result from historical processes far beyond Vietnamese control. But that doesn't make them less of a problem. Social organization is a mundane activity, which Americans take for granted unless they happen to live abroad and encounter a truly inefficient bureaucracy in action. Government, as those in government know only too well, is, for the most part, not politics but administration. It is not the election campaign, the political meeting, or the legislative debate, but instead the workaday labor of the civil servant to collect the garbage, keep the streets clean, educate the people, watch over their health, run a diplomatic corps, or defend the nation from invasion. Modern government is management that should be rational, efficient, and reasonably attractive to the populace. It is bureaucracy in the proper meaning of the word: government by bureau. It requires competence and, above all, sound organization. The greatest of all dangers, as the French say, is the danger of *le système*. Lack of system is the central fact of life about today's society and politics in Vietnam. Ever since the French left, Vietnam has suffered a serious shortage of technically trained civil servants. It has not been the lack of motivation, patriotism, or dedication, nor the limits of technology or capital, but insufficient managerial capacity that has perpetuated the anarchic condition in South Vietnam. We are concerned here with a technical problem—not a reflection on the abilities of Vietnamese as individuals—namely with a system that is inadequate in its ability to engage in planning, forecasting, team leadership, decision making, and follow-through, because it lacks a sufficient number of individuals with necessary managerial skills and experience.

In old Vietnam there was a narrow system for recruitment into government; under the mandarin system those in power tended to recruit from their own groups, and thus administration became a sort of subculture. Government work was not regarded as a means of carrying out programs or solving problems. There was no Puritan-in-politics tradition, no sense of obligation. No one went into government to become a civil "servant." Much of this attitude carries over today and strongly influences the present system. The bureaucrat in Vietnam is system-oriented, not program-oriented, and he tends to see government chiefly as an avenue to success, a means of getting rewards from society.

The French administrative system in Cochin China was almost pure French—French province chiefs, French district chiefs, and even, in some cases, French village chiefs—and French nationals managed affairs and held all the key positions in government. After Dien Bien Phu these administrators sold what they could of their personal belongings and fled, leaving behind what can be described only as an incredible mess. They left just about as total an organizational vacuum as is possible in a society.

The new Vietnamese government, as would be expected, lacked organizational skill at the top and administrative skills at all lower levels. It faced, and still faces, a critical shortage of administrative civil servants. The Vietnamese are bright, talented, competent, and hardworking people, but a corps of trained administrators cannot be created over night, nor even in a decade. Not only does the GVN have the problem of the missing manager, but it also has the problem of a very small recruitment pool. Blame for this lies with the NLF. Because the NLF leaders are by nature organizational animals and because such success as they have enjoyed has been due to the organizational *apparat* at work, they place great priority on countering the South Vietnamese government's organizational efforts and select as chief targets those with organizational or managerial skills. In the villages of Vietnam the NLF has chosen as special targets the natural village leaders, those individuals who do not necessarily hold office but who, because of age, sagacity, or strength of character, are the ones to whom people turn for advice and look to for leadership. They may be religious figures, schoolteachers, or simply people of integrity and honor. Because they are superior individuals, these people are more likely to have the courage to stand up to the NLF when they come to their village and thus are most likely to be the first victims of NLF terror. Potential opposition leadership is the NLF's most deadly enemy. Steadily, quietly, and with a systematic ruthlessness, the NLF in eight years wiped out virtually a whole class of Vietnamese villagers. Many villages today are depopulated of natural leaders, perhaps the single most important element in any society. This represents a human resource of incalculable value. The loss to Vietnam is inestimable, and the country will continue to pay for this genocide for a full generation. Of course, the young each year move into the society, but the Vietnamese regard governing as a function of age, and a twenty-two-year-old boy simply cannot become a village leader.

The basic social structure of Vietnam also contributes to the organizational weakness. Extremely powerful in Vietnam are a host of traditional-type organizations, which are part social, part political, and part religious, such as the Cao Dai or the Hoa Hao. Unfortunately they are largely unsuited for national development, being unlimited rather than specifically defined, with generalized, diffused interests and obligations. The strongest original social group, beyond the family, of course, was the clan, or more accurately the *ho*, the patrilineal lineage. A man's *ho* consisted of all the descendants, through the male line of his patrilineal great-great-grandfather. Usually the *ho* was a rather large body of related persons with a strong sense of identity, often also tied together by economic interests. The *ho* itself gave rise to the "protective association" concept, much like the *tong* in Chinese communities in the United States. Its task was to protect the individual member. It did this not by seeking to change laws or imperial rescripts but by manipulating the court representative—chiefly the tax collector—when he came to the village. From this concept grew a host of protective organizations: the Elderly Buddhist Women's Association, the Ever-Normal Granary Association, burial associations, guilds, wrestling clubs, etc. The French, encountering these groups, suspected them and sought to suppress many of them, giving further impetus to clandestinism. The NLF patterned its "liberation associations" on those early protective associations. The Diem governmental policy was to license and keep under tight control all social organizations, when not entirely discouraging them. The post-Diem governments, realizing they must move to fill an organizational vacuum, have reversed this Diem government policy. Organizational efforts by the government at the village level are of two types: authoritative, namely the bureaucracy and the military, and nonauthoritative, such as farm cooperatives, women's and youth groups, religious organizations, and the various organizations of the Revolutionary Development program. Special RD cadres help villagers establish these organizations, while other cadres work to expedite affairs with the government, arbitrate local disputes, and take the lead in local constructive works. Political action teams, grievance cadres, information teams, drama teams, *Chieu Hoi* teams (which try to persuade villagers to encourage their sons and relatives in the Viet Cong ranks to quit), as well as several other specialized teams reinforce the work of the RD teams. In just a few years Vietnam has seen a proliferation of private social organizations and movements, especially among the young. Trade unions, staunchly and intelligently anti-Communist, are increasing in importance, with a considerable assist from American trade-union leaders. Farm cooperatives are growing steadily. Hardly a day passes that the Saigon press does not report formation of some new special-interest group among farmers, youth, veterans, women, businessmen, and others. The work that these groups do in the villages is limited because of the danger of NLF countermeasures. The wonder is that any forward movement at all is achieved in the face of such opposition.

Legitimatizing Politics

The chief political task facing Vietnam is legitimatizing political power and ending the long night of underground and clandestine politics. In fact, war and peace — certainly the struggle between the NLF and the GVN — can be defined in these terms. Unfortunately, and perhaps this is the principal reason why there is a war in Vietnam in the first place, the Vietnamese have little experience in equitably handling political disputes. Political competition still is seen as a challenge to the central government, requiring stern central government countermeasures. Opposition still is regarded as revolutionary since in the past usually it was, this being the only route to power. Vietnam must learn to legitimatize and make acceptable various political differences, to substitute healthy competitive politics for guerrilla war.

Before the French the political structure in Vietnam was triangular, and no one side directly faced the other two: the Emperor in Hué, the semiautonomous village run by the Council of Elders, and the extended family. Confrontation or even competition was not in the scheme of things. Some political conflict did take place within each of the three elements, chiefly at the court level, where it was politics for insiders only. Village government existed but had no basis in power. The court was decisive. There was no local autonomy except by fact of isolation, no sense of "our rights." Such political activity as did exist in the village was personalized, the politics of entourage, the politics of prestige, with the test being who had the status. Any challenge was personal affront to the leader himself. This has become today's heritage, and the problem now is how to offer political opposition without being considered rebellious or unpatriotic.

The heart of the legitimatization problem is not one of goals, not *what* should be created, but *how*, that is, the rules of the game. Both the NLF and the GVN stand for political modernization. An analysis of the NLF's 1967 Program (cited earlier) and the new GVN constitution shows little difference in social or political goals. Indeed, it seems reasonable to state empirically that, nationalistic sensitivities notwithstanding, if *any nation* is to become modern, certain things must happen: the population must be politically mobilized and engaged; a code-based government of considerable capacity must be developed and must operate rationally, efficiently, and with reasonable attractiveness to the populace; concern must be generated for egalitarianism; differentiated and specialized social movements and organizations, both governmental and private, must be created; and so forth. Although neither the NLF Program nor the GVN Constitution uses the language of the preceding statement, substantively both are in harmony with it.

The basic question is this: How are politics in Vietnam to be made legitimate, and what will be the ultimate configuration of this new form? This problem thus goes far beyond the simple quarrel between the NLF and the GVN — which, after all, is relatively elemental, who gets what power? — and goes deep into the Vietnamese political psyche. It involves centuries of bad political habits. It involves a style and form of politics deeply ingrained into the culture, now almost totally anachronistic.

Thus the foreigner's obvious answer to Vietnamese political problems — to use the franchise and hold an election — is as inadequate as it is obvious. Unfortunately it is not so simple. The ideal of democracy is a weakly held sentiment among almost all the people in Vietnam. This has always been the case, and it remains so today. Few Vietnamese strongly favor Western-style democracy, and if anything the number grows steadily smaller with the passing of each year. Certainly few feel driven to fight to obtain it, or to fight to sustain it. Both knowledge and appreciation of democracy are largely absent. In fact, historically Vietnam has gravitated consistently toward benevolent despotism. It has never known a society with countervailing forces — merchants, traders, clergy, local gentry — which might have been a check on the Emperor and his mandarins or might eventually have moved the country toward a democratic form of government. Buttinger describes this narrow condition, in which there was too little to work with to create a modern state:

> The absence of any group of people other than the mandarins who exercised power or had any means to influence the government's decisions was indeed one of the most striking features of Vietnamese society prior to French intervention. . . . This society without feudal landowners and industrial capitalists, in which the nobility had no political influence and the army no chance to rule, also lacked a body of men with power derived from religion. . . . There [was no] organized church.[6]

The theoretical base was the Confucian ethic: the ruler as a model figure, forever setting the proper example, acting as a strong moral influence. The Emperor meddled as little as possible with the lives of the people within the bamboo hedge of the village. He ruled through superior virtue, which others were moved to emulate, thus obviating the necessity for a tension-building countervailing force system. Two political units, without intervening apparatus, developed. The village became one political unit, the court-mandarin structure the other.

The village was administered (with almost total authority in matters within the village) by the Council of Notables, or Council of Elders, as it is sometimes translated. The council, composed of persons who elsewhere would be known as gentry, made and executed laws within the village, administered village-owned property (of which there might be a great deal), collected and spent taxes, managed public works, adjudicated disputes between families, and generally kept peace within the village. Not only did the council also perform religious rites, but there was a distinct Confucian overtone to its activities. At its head was a *ly truong* (roughly, mayor), although the eldest member

[6] Joseph Buttinger, *The Smaller Dragon* (New York: Praeger, 1958), pp. 283–285.

of the council rather than the *ly truong* normally had the most prestige and influence. It was co-optative: replacements were chosen by the council from a register of heads of families who owned land or through other means had social status. Members served for life without pay.

There was no political participation by the individual villager in the decisions made by the council. Neither was the individual involved in the court-mandarin structure. In fact, the individual almost never dealt directly with the national government; if he had some business to transact, it was handled for him by his village officials. Neither was there any intervening authority or political institution between the village council and the court—for example, no legislative or deliberative body. The mandarin, who stood between the court and the village, was part of the court system, appointed by the Emperor to serve at his pleasure; therefore, he was simply an extension of the Emperor's authority. Nevertheless, this was not a tyrannical system. The Emperor—although supreme in all matters, whether political, military, or religious—was hedged in by tradition, custom, ancient laws, social principles, and expectations of behavior. He ruled by virtue of the "Mandate of Heaven," which Heaven could withdraw, permitting his deposition.

To the individual Vietnamese villager all this was a system of the loosest possible exercise of central power and was representational if not representative government at the local level, with certain built-in restraints at both levels to prevent the worst of governmental excesses. The important point, however, is that it also was a system in which there was no individual political participation. Individuals got virtually no experience with government, certainly none of the educative experiences of a citizen in a democracy. And since the system was not particularly oppressive, there was little to generate a demand for self-determination. In short, there developed no taste and no appetite for democracy.

This is not to deny the existence, past or present, of a strong desire for political participation by villagers at the village level. Extensive research into village attitudes during the past eight years clearly indicates that local self-determination, the right to have a voice in choosing the men that run the village, is one of the four "minimal needs" of the Vietnamese villager.[7] And this desire stems from historical forces as well as obvious rational self-interest. As noted earlier, traditional Vietnamese government at the village level was representational but not representative. The ruling Council of Elders met and selected a new member when a vacancy occurred. There was no election in the village, except in the form of the subtle but very powerful village consensus. For example, Mr. Ba, a member of the council, dies. The consensus of the villagers, let us say, is that Mr. Phu is most worthy of taking Mr. Ba's place. If there were an election, Mr. Phu would be elected. The council members are aware of this sentiment and honor it. If they do not, the repercussions in the village can be drastic: for example, half the villagers may move down the road a few miles to establish a new village there. If there is a genuine difference of opinion—two worthy candidates, say Mr. Phu and Mr. Mai—the matter is quietly arbitrated among Mr. Phu, Mr. Mai, and the council. This is the famed Vietnamese "private arrangement" in politics. It might be agreed, for example, that Mr. Phu would get the

[7] The four are: peace (or security or absence of anxiety); economic opportunity (the so-called revolution of rising expectation); local self-determination; and rule of law (i.e., justice, absence of corruption, a codified form of government as opposed to government by whim).

appointment but that Mr. Mai would fill the next vacancy or that he would be named to some other position of trust in the village. Then the council meets formally and goes through the motion of decision making, although everyone in the village knows what has been arranged. This system is a form of political participation regardless of how it may appear to a foreigner. A Vietnamese villager felt involved; he knew that what he thought and wanted carried weight with the council. At the same time it prevented open political confrontation within the village which could tear the village apart. This sentiment for "private arrangements" in politics remains strong today. Most Vietnamese, North and South alike, if candid, will tell you they are skeptical of the notion that the proper way to divide political power is to have people go into a little booth and drop pieces of paper in a box. This is not the traditional way it has been done in Vietnam. Further, they add, there is something starkly un-Vietnamese about the process. The all-or-nothing, win-lose character of an election ignores the imperative of group harmony, they argue. It tears a society apart, drives the losers to desperate measures because they get nothing, whereas in the traditional Vietnamese system of "private arrangements," the loser would get something. Parenthetically, this suggests that the Vietnamese view of an election is not quite like that of a Western democracy, but that the Vietnamese reaction should not be attributed to indifference, cynicism, or ignorance, as it often is.

It also is worth noting that in the DRV no progress has been made in twenty-three years toward self-government, not even the "winds of liberalism" that ostensibly are blowing through Eastern European countries. The rule in North Vietnam is as harsh, arbitrary, and intrusive as in any totalitarian nation on earth. Because of the lack of heritage that might otherwise put pressure on the state, there is little demand for self-determination among North Vietnamese, little resentment against the state when it intrudes deeply, and little sentiment for the various political freedoms so highly valued in the West. What drive does exist has been absorbed by the state in its various emulation campaigns and in activities at the village level (especially in the village cooperative). But the chief reason is that there is no heritage of democracy—people can hardly miss what they've never had, even historically.

Throughout Vietnam, but primarily in our major concern, the South, one of the chief problems mitigating against legitimatization of politics is clandestinism. This is something far greater than a desire by politicians to politick out of the limelight, or the existence of secret political groups, which are found in all societies. It is a style of politics deeply ingrained in the Vietnamese personality. Clandestinism for 900 years was a means of dealing with the foreign occupier—the Chinese, then the French. But its basis is more fundamental. It rests on the Vietnamese assumption that society consists of a host of dangerous and conflicting social forces with which only the enigmatic organization and a secret "inness" can cope. Power in old Vietnam was something to be fought for, to be seized, and clung to exclusively. No emperor ever willingly shared it. This inevitably gave rise to clandestine politics, which, with the arrival of the French, soon developed into a high art. Vietnam became a labyrinth of intrigue probably never equaled elsewhere. Clandestine politics, the only politics possible, became a way of life. A code of clandestinism developed. It involved methods, unwritten laws, imperatives, mores, and customs, all combining to fix proper political behavior and determine the tradition.

A clandestine organization is made up of two parts, an overt element seen by the world and a covert one known only to the insiders. Both elements are real — the overt one is not simply a front. The Cao Dai is a typical example of such an organization. Founded in 1919 ostensibly as a movement to merge all of the world's religions into one, it was not until 1931 — we know now from an inspection of French *Sûreté* records — that the French became aware that the Cao Dai actually was an anti-French, ultranationalist organization. While it may seem surprising to an outsider that 10 per cent of the people in a colonial nation could be members of an anticolonial organization without the colonizers being aware of their activities, such was the case in Vietnam. A strong effect of clandestinism has been to generate distrust of all political activity as well as a tendency to see politics chiefly as a system of organized betrayal. Vietnamese history is full of accounts of double-dealings among the rulers and indeed public figures at all levels. At times political and even personal betrayal seems almost endemic in the society. One of the author's sage friends once commented, "You could write the history of Vietnam in terms of the double-cross." Frequently over the years the author's Vietnamese friends have asserted that "eventually America will sell us out." When pressed for an explanation for this belief, usually they say something like this: "Everyone sells us out! The Japanese, the French, the Communists twice, Ngo Dinh Diem, the country's intellectuals. All have sold us out! So who are you Americans to be any different?"

The leader in a clandestine organization also marches to a different drum. He is moved by pursuit of the system's special virtues, and he acts within clandestinism's own values. It is well known, for example, that the official leader of the organization is not the holder of real power. But it seems possible that if one is clever, one can penetrate the system and find behind this figurehead the true power holder; only later does one discover that this second figure was, in effect, put there to be discovered and that behind this figure is a third figure (or possibly a fourth or fifth) wielding the real power. The mind boggles. Like peeling an onion, once it is peeled, nothing is left. In any event, the system is in a state of constant mutation, and soon new alliances outdate one's discoveries. The ideal leader of a clandestine organization is he who best stage-manages his group before the public. He is sly, paternalistic, skilled at intrigue, and master of the deceptive move. At the same time he reciprocates loyalty, protects his followers, and achieves for them whatever they seek: power, status, or money. The model clandestine leader in Vietnam, of course, is the man the world calls Ho Chi Minh. We know little about him, and probably much of what we do know is wrong. Of no other important world leader can it be said that we don't know where he was for nearly a decade, the 1930's. Some Vietnamese scholars maintain that the original Ho Chi Minh, or Nguyen Ai Quoc, as he was then known, died in a Hong Kong prison in 1932 (his obituary was carried in the British Communist Party newspaper, *Daily Worker*, on August 11, 1932) and that his place was taken by another Vietnamese who, under his name, went on to become the present-day North Vietnamese leader. Ho Chi Minh has lived under a half-dozen aliases, some of them chosen apparently because they are puns in Chinese. Through the years he has done nothing to clear up the uncertainties of his past and in fact has given interviewers a wide variety of accounts of his life. In the tradition of clandestinism, he behaves exactly as a good leader should, by throwing sand in the eyes of the world.

For a follower in a clandestine organization there also is a kind of model behavior. He must be in step with the movement, change when it changes. He must know when to be loyal and when the time for loyalty has passed. He never takes an irretrievable position, never makes a final commitment. Certainly no one ever takes him for granted. Proselyting is common, and no opprobrium exists with respect to changing sides, providing one observes a decent interval. Loyalty may be a virtue, but consistency is not. Nor is there a strong stigma against the traitor in Vietnam. Most Vietnamese of middle age or older have been on all sides of all political issues.

Obviously, clandestinism is appropriate in dealing with an occupation force but irrelevant when governing oneself. The sad truth is that Vietnamese politicians, at least of the old school, *like* clandestinism and are frankly bored by orthodox politics, open decisions openly arrived at in the course of parliamentary debate. The new politics in Saigon is constitutional politics, but the old professionals still engage in a sort of self-canceling political intrigue that no one, except perhaps foreigners, takes very seriously.

Though Vietnamese politics tend toward the traditional, are divisive, and have a peculiar style of their own, they are not politics of oligarchy. There is not the "50 families running the country" problem that plagues certain South American and Middle Eastern countries. Political mobility exists. Actually Vietnam has always had a fairly mobile political system, the mandarin and court system was a world difficult but not impossible to enter. It required tutelage, but occasionally a village collectively would finance the education of a particularly bright boy. If he passed the written examination of the Confucian classics, he could in one leap be part of the court-mandarin system. There was perhaps less political mobility under the French than at any time in Vietnamese history. Once the French hold was broken, no old guard took over. There quickly emerged new power blocks, led by people from previously powerless classes. This tendency has been accelerated in the past few years: the Buddhists, the youth, the military — these are the vanguard in the new political mobility. This fact is not well appreciated outside of Vietnam where the tendency of even well-informed persons is to view the power elite in Vietnam as the "same old vested interests of the French days."

In an effort to determine political mobility in Vietnam the author conducted an informal study, the results of which appear in Table 2-1. It is an investigation of the social back-

TABLE 2-1

1967 Political Mobility Study (Social Background)

Middle-class business		24%
Civil servant[a]		20%
Landowner[b]		14%
Education		10%
Elementary-secondary	8%	
University	2%	
Mandarin[c]		8%
Medicine		6%
Law-judiciary		4%
Other		2%
Not available		12%
	Total	100%

[a] For the most part *fonctionnaire* or *duc phu su* during French colonial days; but not mandarin or royal blood.

[b] In some cases landowners but generally estate owners or gentry.

[c] Includes a few individuals of royal blood.

ground and status ladder of the most powerful and influential of today's Vietnamese personalities. The list of the Vietnamese studied was developed in two ways: the names appearing in *Who's Who in Vietnam*, a biographic handbook issued by the Vietnam Press Agency in Saigon, were listed; and the author asked eleven of his most politically knowledgeable Vietnamese friends to list in no particular order the "ten most powerful men in Vietnam." (There were no further instructions, and no definition of "powerful" was offered.) The result was a 126-name list to which the author added seven names that he considered important but that were not on either list. The final list of 130 names[8] was then surveyed. Two questions were asked: What is the person's social background in terms of the occupation of his father? What occupational ladder did the individual use in his climb to power?

The most common background for a Vietnamese power holder today is a middle-class family (24 per cent), followed by individuals whose fathers were civil servants (that is, *fonctionnaires* or *duc phu su*) under the French (20 per cent), but not of mandarin or royal background. Next came the "landowners," who can be landlords with great holdings or simply families that lived on rural estates, that is, gentry (14 per cent). The rest—education, mandarin, medicine, law-judiciary—were less than 10 per cent each. About 12 per cent remain unaccounted for. In the case of the Vietnam Press Agency publication, this strongly suggests middle- or lower-class background, since a person with such a background would be hesitant to state it in such a publication. It is interesting to note that not a single individual came, or said he came, from a military family. The social background

[8] Three names were eliminated in the course of the study (circa early 1967, one the result of death and two because they had been removed from office; the latter perhaps is a commentary on the degree of power held by any Vietnamese, since the two removed were military corps commanders who had been summarily dismissed from what had seemed to be impregnable political positions.

breakdown is about what one would expect in Vietnam. Peasants as yet simply do not rise to positions of power. Political power still resides in the hands of offspring of the 10 or 15 per cent of the population able to prepare their sons for the assumption of power principally through a Western education. The exceptions to this are certain Buddhists.

The second part of the study sought to analyze the ladder each individual used in his ascendance to power. (See Table 2-2.) The largest single group was the professional

TABLE 2-2
1967 Social Mobility Study (Ladder of Rise)

Professional military		22%
University[a]		18%
Religion		18%
Buddhist	7%	
Sects[b]	6%	
Catholic[c]	5%	
Business		18%
Law-judiciary		13%
Journalism		6%
Diplomacy		5%
	Total	100%

[a] Faculty members of universities who considered themselves academicians even though at the time in government service.
[b] Cao Dai and Hoa Hao religious sects.
[c] Includes members of the clergy in academic assignments.

military (22 per cent), followed by university professionals (18 per cent), religionists (18 per cent), and businessmen (18 per cent). The law and the judiciary, collectively, accounted for the next most common route (13 per cent), followed by journalism (6 per cent) and diplomacy (5 per cent). This breakdown suggests that the route to power in Vietnam is fairly evenly spread among the armed forces, religion, the academic and business worlds.

This, of course, was a gross study and provided no weighting for degrees of power held by individuals. This was not its purpose. Its purpose was simply to inspect social mobility. Following are some conclusions based on the study's findings: It is not true that "those who held power in the French days still hold it." Quite the opposite. Those individuals or families who were powerful under the French or under the court in Hué are rare in today's politics. The background of most power holders is middle class. The "big rich" are not common among them. Neither are the poor or the peasants. The chief advantage enjoyed by today's power holder, which enables him to rise, is that he came from an educated family. Educated parents appear to be far more important than rich families. The self-made man is rare. No single background is of particular advantage in becoming a power holder. Likewise, no single ladder to status is dominant. In fact, in both cases, the chief characteristic is multiplicity.

Prospects

The intent in this chapter on Vietnam's political and social milieu has been not to generate pessimism but to encourage realism. Vietnam's problems are not insurmountable. In fact, much of the activity described adds up to progress. After years in a political deep-freeze Vietnam is beginning to make progress toward constitutionalism. This indeed is a revolution. Government in traditional Vietnam was government by whim. The law was what the Emperor said was the law that morning. There was little impersonal justice, virtually no codified government or what we today would call rule of law. Ngo Dinh Diem moved South Vietnam toward constitutional government: during his regime a constitution was promulgated. But increasingly Diem came to rely on administrative controls and bypassed the National Assembly as well as the Constitution. After Diem, Vietnam went through a period of public disorders in which there was first, in effect, government by *coup d'état* and then, also in effect, government by street demonstration. This was followed by a somewhat more orderly system, the Military Directorate, which governed by means of what were called decree laws (*sac luat*) and departmental orders (*nghi dinh*), which had the effect of laws but actually were executive orders. Only in mid-1966 did Vietnam begin to move toward a true constitutional government.

Probably it is a political dictum that in creating a constitutional government the first step is the hardest and each successive step is progressively easier. Once events are moving, a kind of momentum sets in that tends to reduce—but of course never eliminates—the obstacles to success. Certainly, in the first step, the various elections held in late 1966 and in 1967 (Constituent Assembly elections; the Presidential and Legislative elections) were so fraught with danger that their success impressed even the most cynical observer. The Vietnamese Constitution, as a document, can hardly be faulted. It recognizes and guarantees the basic human rights and freedoms of its citizens; it delineates power functions among the legislative, executive, and judicial branches of government; it is secular; it provides for universal franchise; it goes beyond many constitutions in establishing a legalized base for social welfare programs; it protects minority groups; its provisions for the legislative and judicial systems are sound; it provides for the first time in Vietnam a legal base for local self-determination; it provides for and protects political parties, social movements, labor unions, and other private social and political organizations; it is open-ended in that it permits amendment. In general, it establishes a firm governmental structure, divides power within the government, and creates an arena in which regional interests, religious organizations, social and political groups can legitimately act out the drama of politics. Important as it is, however, the fact of the Constitution should not be exaggerated, for good constitutions are easy to come by, but the test is in making the document a real and vital force. Even so, the 1966–1968 elections have begun to change to a degree the pattern of Vietnamese politics. There has been a sorting out of the numerous "political tendencies" in Saigon, making politics somewhat more manageable. The status of the civilian politician has been raised. The groundwork has been laid for meaningful participation in politics at the Saigon level. Beyond this must come the extension of the political process to the provincial level, then to the district, and finally to the rice roots, the village.

One useful way of looking at politics in South Vietnam is to regard the present government in Saigon as a coalition government and the NLF as a sort of disloyal opposition. The GVN is not a coalition in the European sense, that is, composed of known modern political parties such as the Social Democrats, Radical Socialists, Christian Democrats. Instead it is a coalition of traditional mutual-protection organizations, partly social and partly political. The chief such groups and their percentages of the total population are: Roman Catholics (8 per cent); Hoa Hao (8 per cent); overseas Chinese (6 per cent), with considerable economic power; montagnards (6 per cent), with only slight involvement; Cao Dai (5 per cent); activist Buddhists (4 per cent); government *fonctionnaires* or old-line civil servants, called *duc phu su* (3 per cent); the khaki force, chiefly military officers (3 per cent); the Dai Viets (2 per cent); the Vietnam Quoc Dan Dang (2 per cent);[9] and other groups that are influential but numerically small, such as the trade-union movement, students, Protestants, and the intellectual community. This totals approximately half the adult population.[10] Another third represents the most traditional-minded villagers, still largely outside the national political process. Facing this coalition is the NLF, representing perhaps at most 15 per cent of the population.

Serious political activity in Vietnam is not found in legislative debate, election speeches, or even in political party activities, but in the work of these major social, political, and religious organizations. Here is where the real power resides. The mutual-protection association is the basic unit of politics in Vietnam and will remain so in the foreseeable future. Moreover, it will continue to be the political target, the real political prize. To measure politics in Vietnam, it will be necessary to study the strengths, strategies, and interrelationships of the various mutual-protection associations. The legislature, for example, should be viewed in light of the words and votes of the representatives of these organizations. The individual speaking for his group is what really counts—not the charismatic individual, not the geographic-area representative (although region will be reflected), and certainly not the policy-oriented ideologue. Government will continue to be what it is now, a coalition of traditional-type social movements. As these groups interact with one another, especially in the legislature, the Vietnamese politician will move to the forefront and become a key figure. He becomes the broker who puts together the political mix acceptable

[9] For description of the two elitist political parties, the VNQDD and the Dai Viets, see Douglas Pike, *Viet Cong* (Cambridge, Mass.: The M.I.T. Press, 1966), Chapters 1 and 2.

[10] These percentages are not meant to be precise; they are used simply to illustrate the nature of political groups in Vietnam today.

to all groups. The groups, or their spokesmen, seek him out, make their requests, their pleas, their demands. He then balances the pro groups, the anti groups, the swing groups and makes his decision. The system modernizes the group just as it enhances the elected politician. We have seen in Vietnam in the past few years a surge of effort in this special-interest group process. It has contributed to the development of a system of specific social and political institutions with precisely formulated roles, modern rather than traditional kinds of organizations. Vietnamese are becoming familiar with specifically defined interest groups. Eventually, the NLF, or at least members of the NLF, will be integrated into this political decision-making arena. Since it is trying to get into the arena now, the problem is not how to bring it in, but how to allow it what it has a right to have, a share of the power, without allowing it what it now wants, and has no right to, which is a monopoly of power. Many of the wisest Vietnamese envision as the interim political configuration for Vietnam what they term the one-and-a-half-party system. In this system the "one" party represents all or nearly all the major groups in the country, and the "half" party incorporates the more radical elements with extremist views (including elements of the NLF) and serves as a safety valve, giving members a vent for their feelings, as well as having a leavening effect on politics.

What does this mean with respect to the three Weberian types of leaders: the traditional, the charismatic, and the rational-legal? Traditional leadership has proved unequal to the needs of Vietnam; that was the meaning of the career of Ngo Dinh Diem. The charismatic leader, while theoretically possible for Vietnam, seems unlikely; the Vietnamese are too cynical not to suspect a leader of his charisma, too distrusting to grant him the power he would seek, indeed should have. This leaves the rational-legal type of leader, and that type probably will be the coming, future leader; but he will not appear as a full type until clandestinism has to a considerable degree burned itself out.

The machinery itself has been created; now the machine must be made to run. Many troubles lie ahead, but at least Vietnam is getting organized. Of course, the final mix will be authentically Vietnamese, or it will not endure. Vietnam will define and work out the details. Heritage will continue to limit her, and she will continue to be the victim of the historical accident. The process will be no neat and tidy one, particularly while the fighting continues. But all that is past and all that will come will be instructive. Perhaps ultimately that is what political development is all about: thrusting people into tasks that must be done, depending on them to devise solutions for problems that seemed insoluble when they set them for themselves. As was wisely noted long ago, trust the people with the gravest questions, and in the end you educate the human race.

CHAPTER THREE

PROGNOSIS WITHOUT PREDICTION

This chapter will attempt to suggest the general directions that events in Vietnam can take as the country moves toward eventual peace. What appears here is a sorting-out process, following eight years of warfare, of the way things can go, a discussion confined to possibilities and prospects. *There is no intent to predict the future of Vietnam.* Most published considerations of Vietnam's future delimit the options open to the combatants: expand the war by heavy bombing of all North Vietnam; withdraw unilaterally; intensify the land war in the South; make an all-out diplomatic assault effort for a negotiated settlement; concentrate Allied military forces in coastal enclaves; compel a political settlement; or some other option. Usually these choices are presented to us in such a way that all are unacceptable except the one that the speaker or author happens to favor. In any event, this simplistic pigeonholing does injustice to reality. Vietnam, first and foremost, is complex, and the permutations of its complexities are overwhelming. Consider some of the factors: the military dimension within Vietnam, strategy versus strategy, divisions within each strategy within each camp; the accident of battles won or lost; the involuted politics of the DRV Politburo; events in Vietnam automatically affecting internal politics and external relations of countries around the world, many of them not even involved in the war; the power struggle in China; the Sino-Soviet dispute; the "fresh winds" of Eastern Europe; American social pathology; American politics; the capitalist world's currency troubles; the historical conjuncture or accident; the nearly intolerable frustrations that at times plague all, on both sides. It follows, then, that with this great interaction of complex factors, it is impossible to predict events in Vietnam beyond a few months. Still — and this is not a contradiction — it is possible to circumnavigate the subject and outline the straits into which events, of necessity, must be channeled.

The Continuum

These channels are portrayed here by means of a schematic diagram (see Figure 3-1) conceived as a continuum. At one end of the continuum is Decisive Victory (or Defeat), at the other is Accommodation (primarily of the NLF, but in the long run also of the DRV). To the right along the continuum a point is reached where two routes to Accommodation are open: one via the conference table, that is, through formal, legalistic, public, and international negotiations, the other through private arrangements that are closed, informal, individualized, and strictly Vietnamese. The diagram could be extended to the left past Decisive Victory (or Defeat) to what might be termed total victory or unconditional surrender. However, an inspection of the way in which wars of the second half of the twentieth century have ended indicates that the fuzzy and unclear outcome is far more likely than a clean-cut total victory. Theoretically it is possible that events in Vietnam could shuttle back and forth along the midsection of the con-

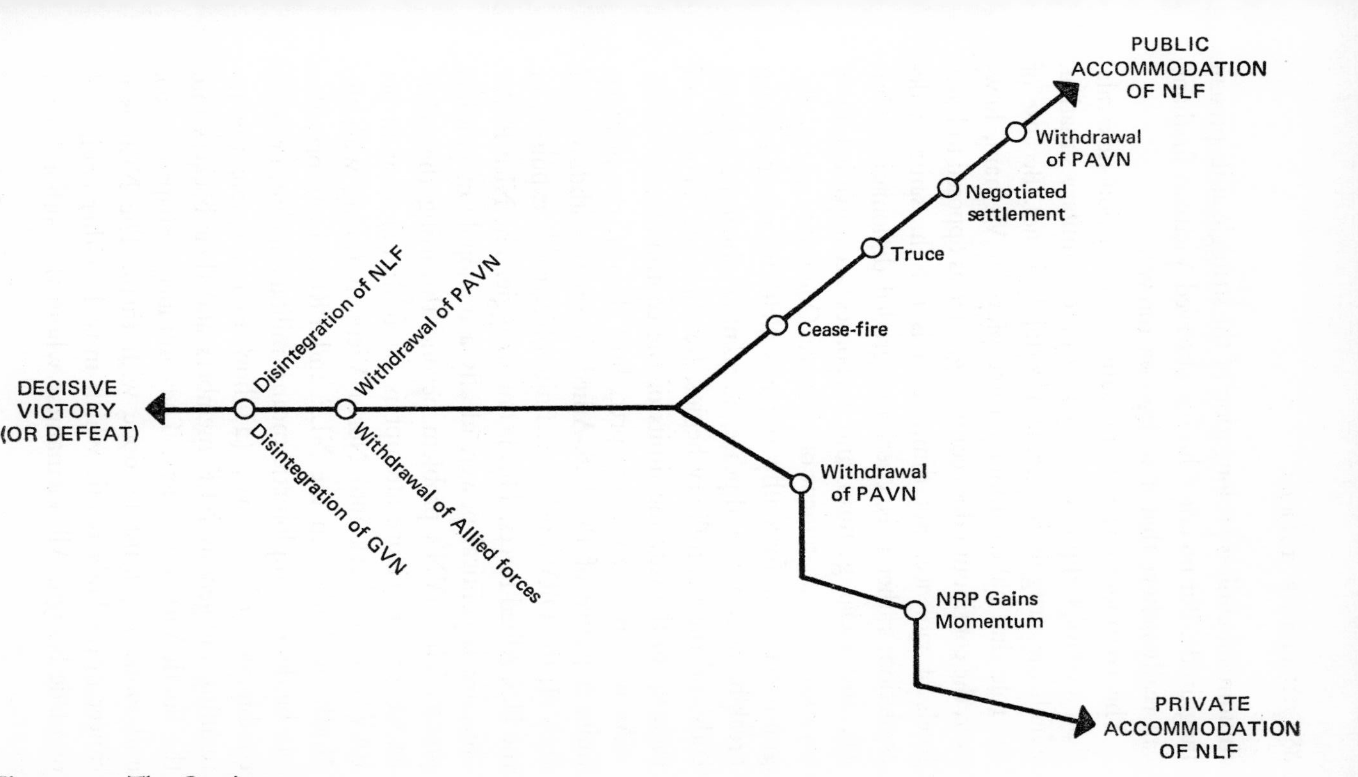

Figure 3-1 The Continuum

tinuum, an endless prolongation of the struggle at its present magnitude. But no one who has observed Vietnam firsthand can really believe that it will go on forever.

The continuum is not the same as escalation–de-escalation, a concept applicable only to a purely military situation, which the struggle in Vietnam certainly is not. Because of the role that naked military force plays in Vietnam, however, the continuum does connote greater as opposed to lesser levels of violence. But diminution is not the same as de-escalation; rather it is a series of graded diplomatic, political, and social gestures and responses accompanied by a corresponding abatement of violence. One utility of this diagram is that it forcefully suggests that there is no sharp break between war and peace, no point at which the military ends and the nonmilitary begins, for there are elements of each up to the extreme limits of the continuum.

As we have seen in the preceding chapter, the primary, finite objective of the U.S.-Allied forces is withdrawal of PAVN; the DRV's primary, finite objective is expulsion of the U.S.-Allied forces. This is one struggle. The NLF-PLAF objective is political power, ideally a monopoly of political power. The GVN's problem beyond thwarting the NLF-PLAF power seizure attempt is twofold: (1) how to get PAVN troops back into North Vietnam (along with the Northern civilians in the NLF and PRP); in theory, this can be done by diplomatic means, military means, or some combination of the two; (2) how to reintegrate the remaining indigenous NLF members and their backers into the South Vietnam society. They number perhaps 750,000, and *something* must be done with them. The NLF is a cancer in the body politic which must be either eradicated or made benign. All Vietnamese whom the author knows believe that eventually the NLF members will and must be accommodated.

From the DRV-PRP viewpoint, there is a single problem: how to unite North and South Vietnam. The imponderable here is whether the DRV would settle for some sort of unification that would neither involve the use of force nor require Northern, that is, Communist, dominance.

For a Southerner in the NLF there is a single problem: how to achieve political power. It seems clear that the individual NLF member who is not a dedicated Marxist (and few of them know or care much about Communist ideology, even those professing to be Communists) seeks essentially the same goals as to the Vietnamese who support the GVN. The NLF member, if divested of NLF control, would be free to search for a political framework in which he could strive for the democracy, justice, and other virtues that, he says, represent his cause. As we shall see later, the GVN began a strategy in mid-1968 designed to accommodate the NLF members as individuals but not as members of the NLF. From the viewpoint of anyone outside the Vietnam scene, in suggesting a solution to the Vietnam problem the chief task is to devise a workable formula for converting this zero-sum game into a non-zero-sum game.

Peace via Decisive Victory or Defeat

If events move to the left on the continuum toward Decisive Victory, we shall see, if it is GVN-Allied victory, the withdrawal of PAVN probably through fade-out, the disintegration of the NLF as a coherent organization (but not physical destruction of its members), withdrawal of U.S.-Allied forces, and then perhaps a decade of steadily declining low-level guerrilla war by remnants of the NLF-PRP in the back country, where it would not seriously interfere with the business of nation building. If events were to go toward Decisive Victory for the DRV-NLF, we would see early withdrawal of U.S.-Allied forces, the disintegration of the GVN and a quick takeover by the NLF-DRV, the gradual withdrawal of PAVN, and the amalgamation of North and South Vietnam at whatever rate seemed feasible to the Hanoi leaders with regard to world public opinion at the time. Should events move to the continuum's left, the question of military strategy obviously will be all-important. The military role will continue to be a dominant one and certainly, at certain times, decisive. The question of strategy is so complex, so deeply rooted in what has gone before—that is, past strategies—as to require separate consideration. Chapter Four is devoted entirely to this subject.

Peace via Accommodation

If events move to the right on the continuum, we shall see either early or late withdrawal of PAVN and U.S.-Allied troops, the accommodation of the NLF either through diplomatic negotiations or through private arrangements. The political models for these two routes to accommodation are, in the case of the conference table route, the end of the Viet Minh war at the 1954 Geneva Conference. The closest available model for private accommodation is Greece in the 1940's or Malaya in the late 1950's.

What is involved in accommodation—and perhaps the term is ill chosen—is ending present polarization in Vietnamese society. South Vietnam now has two more or less separate political processes at work, the NLF and GVN. Neither can be removed from the scene. Yet as long as the polarization remains, the society will continue to be unstable. What is required, obviously, is the creation of a single political sphere. The task — and this has been the task since the start of the insurgency — is to separate the authentic, indigenous Southern elements in the NLF from the Northerners and then to integrate the Southerners on a fair-share basis. Most Vietnamese who think much about the problem believe that after a burning-out phase of military activity accommodation will begin, either through the conference table or by means of what is here termed private accommodation. The two roads are not, of course, mutually exclusive. But, in analysis, it is useful to think of them separately, for in operation, they are separate processes. Both are now underway.

Public Accommodation. The matter of accommodation by means of a formal international conference is considered in Chapter Four. One aspect of such a negotiated settlement relevant to accommodation is discussed here: *coalition government.*

On the surface, the suggestion of a coalition government in South Vietnam would seem a straightforward proposal, at least in theory. As is often the case with Vietnam, that which should be the simplest is the most complicated. And the complexity here is one of the most difficult kinds: it is linguistic. Outsiders use the term "coalition government" in a clear-cut way, meaning a European-style political power-sharing arrangement by going political parties. The mere term in Vietnamese has multiple meaning. Beyond this it has special meaning to the NLF and the DRV. In order to explain this it is necessary to plunge into Vietnamese semantics. Here it should be noted parenthetically that Vietnamese is a subtle language with a deliberately high ambiguity level;

the Vietnamese often use their language not to reveal but to obscure.

In its 1960 Manifesto, the NLF called for the creation of a "broad, national democratic coalition government . . . [to include] representatives of all strata of the people, of all nationalities, political parties and religious communities and of patriotic parties and of patriotic personalities." This is the wording used by the NLF in its English-language version of its Manifesto circulated in South Vietnam in 1960; also it is the wording used by the DRV in its official English-language version published subsequently in Hanoi. In some versions of the Manifesto appearing in the United States, however, the term "broad, national democratic coalition government" (*chanh quyen lien minh dan toc dan chu*)[1] has been translated "a government of national democratic union." In its 1967 Program the NLF (in its own translation into English) called for the creation of a "national union democratic government (*chanh phu lien hiep dan toc va dan chu*). The important difference in these two phrases, and between the 1960 Manifesto and the 1967 Program, is found in the differing use of two terms: *lien minh,* which appeared in the 1960 Manifesto, and *lien hiep,* which was used in the 1967 Program. Compounding the confusion is the fact that during the past generation sharp differences in word usage, semantic meanings, and grammar have developed between Vietnamese as it is spoken in Hanoi and Vietnamese as it is spoken in Saigon.[2] This can mean differing translations into English of the same Vietnamese word depending

[1] Literally, state structure (i.e., power or authority) alliance national democratic.

[2] In part due to the DRV effort to de-Sinoize the Vietnamese language by eliminating from usage as many words with a Chinese root as possible, in favor of those of purely Vietnamese origin.

on whether the translator is working in Hanoi or Saigon. In Saigon the term *lien minh* is translated as "alliance" but also is used to describe a coalition arrangement in an alliance or common-front sense, as in such (South) Vietnamese terms as *lien minh cong nong* (worker-peasant alliance) or *lien minh quoc te* (international alliance). Hanoi translates *lien minh* as "coalition." In Saigon *lien hiep* is used in terms denoting government organizations, as for example the Vietnamese term for the United Nations (*Lien Hiep Quoc*). The NLF in its 1960 Manifesto used the term *lien minh* and translated it as "coalition government." In its 1967 Program it used the term *lien hiep* and translated this as "union."[3] Thus from a literal reading of these two documents in English, it would seem correct to say that in 1960 the NLF stood for coalition government but in 1967 it did not (or by 1967 it was saying it stood for a *union* government rather than coalition government, which, if nothing else, in English raises the level of ambiguity).

Yet we cannot let our consideration of the term "coalition government" rest here. Denotation also enters. Simply stated, the NLF-PRP-DRV definition of "coalition government" is quite different from the definition in Europe or the United States. To the DRV and the NLF there is in South Vietnam first and foremost the great mass of the people. They are represented by the NLF, the "sole legitimate representative of the South Vietnamese people," as the NLF usually describes itself. Second, there are bourgeois sociopolitical groups, such as the Catholics, who are not part of the NLF. Finally, there is a third entity, the GVN. The NLF call for a coalition government is defined as a government that does

[3] The Rumanians in December 1967 circulated their version of the NLF 1967 Program at the United Nations; in it *lien hiep* was translated into English as "coalition government."

not include the GVN but in which sociopolitical groups, such as the Catholics, are represented; that is, their voices could be heard in council but they would not hold actual power. The power would be reserved for NLF as the sole, legitimate representative of the people (the idea is somewhat akin to the early Communist notion that defined the proletariat as the only legitimate power holder, thus justifying the "dictatorship" of the proletariat, that is, its monopolization of power). The NLF theoreticians see nothing inconsistent with the assertion that a South Vietnam coalition government would not — could not — include present cabinet members of the GVN. To the NLF, the GVN is a "disguised colonial regime set up by the U.S. imperialists, a servile administration which must be overthrown."[4] It is not an entity with which it could associate politically. In short, the NLF flatly refuses to share power with President Thieu or members of his cabinet. The "coalition government" that it would find acceptable would be one in which the NLF held power and in which the interests of various social and religious groups in South Vietnam would be considered. These were defined in 1960 as "every sector of the population, various nationalities, political parties, religious communities and patriotic personalities."[5]

In its 1967 Program the elements with which the NLF would associate itself were "the most representative persons among the various social strata, nationalities, religious communities, patriotic and democratic parties, patriotic personalities and forces which have contributed to the cause of the national liberation." Thus there appears to be a delimiting of the groups between 1960 and 1967. The final eleven words of the 1967 quotation, that the NLF would associate with those

[4] The NLF 1960 Manifesto.
[5] *Ibid.*

"*forces which have contributed to the cause of the national liberation,*" presumably mean that anyone who has not so contributed will not share the power. In summary, the NLF sees as its opposition various Vietnamese political groups and religious organizations, as well as the GVN itself. It is willing to deal with the various organizations (that is, see that their interests are represented in the governmental structure, though nothing specific is promised by the NLF); but, in any case, *there would be no participation by the present power holders in Saigon.* This stand appears in almost every NLF statement; ex-NLF cadres interviewed by the author insist that it actually is the stand and is not simply a bargaining position. It seems clear that if the NLF maintains this position, NLF-style coalition government would require elimination of the entire present GVN leadership. Accommodation via the conference table involves negotiating a future role for the NLF in the political life of South Vietnam. To insist that all the political figures on the other side must be excluded from this future—which is what the logic of the NLF position would dictate—would make the prospects for accommodation slight, to say the least.

Private Accommodation. This involves integration privately arrived at, not publicly negotiated, and without announced formal arrangements. The chief difference between the two roads to accommodation, however, is that the public route deals with the NLF as an organization while the private route deals with the NLF members as individuals. Following the former route, the NLF as an organization would assume a role in the decision-making process in South Vietnam (whatever role came out of the bargaining), while by the latter route, the individual members of the NLF (but not their organization) would be integrated into the political arena of South Vietnam. In many ways the issue of the life of the NLF is not a crucial one. What really counts is the future of one NLF organization, the PRP. The NLF as a front organization is composed of a conglomeration of disparate groups and organizations, some real and some kept, with only a minimum of common interests, with no real life of its own, and in any case now dominated by the DRV. The NLF is not monolithic, though it has been treated so over the years. Neither is there any ideological cement holding it together, as is the case with the PRP. Its members have little unanimity of view other than opposition to the GVN and the desire for political power. What held it together in the past, beyond the entrapment qualities of the organization itself, was anticipation of victory. What holds it together now is Northern discipline, exercised by the 20,000 civilian cadres (out of a total NLF cadre strength of 40,000), who are "pure" Northerners.[6]

Private accommodation involves in part an extension, continuation, and refinement of the present GVN policy toward the NLF—which is to offer accommodation to its members but not to the organization itself. Even if events remain favorable for the GVN, this probably will continue to be its policy, at least until the NLF has become so weakened organizationally that the GVN no longer fears direct confrontation with it.

The scenario for public accommodation, as envisioned by its proponents, goes something like this:

The DRV leadership concludes that its present strategy for obtaining unification is not working, and a new strategy

[6] That is, those from the North, whose families are in the North, whose promotions come from the North, who plan to return some day to the North; quite logically they are loyal to the Northern objective of unification.

is ordered (the alternatives are discussed in Chapter Four). Hard-line advocates in the DRV Politburo charge that the new policy is capitulation, but their objections are overridden. One of the results of the new strategy — the only one we are concerned with here — is that the PAVN troops in South Vietnam become irrelevant under the new doctrine. Since they no longer are required, they are withdrawn, probably fading out, not ostentatiously departing. This is seen as the first quantum drop in the magnitude of the war, back to its pre-1965 level. Withdrawal of PAVN, of course, has a deleterious effect on the NLF and to a lesser degree on the PRP. The position of Northern cadres in NLF organizations in parts of the country becomes untenable, and in general they relocate, withdraw to North Vietnam, or attempt to integrate into PLAF units (as, for example, B-40 rocket teams attached to main force PLAF units). A heavy exodus from the cause begins among the NLF supporters, particularly those on the perimeter of the circle (see Figure 3-2). That many would abandon the ship has been anticipated by the leaders, who tell themselves that they are well rid of unreliable faint-hearts and that the organization, though smaller, is stronger for it. But this loss of personnel reduces the level of combat that PLAF can sustain. The result is a second quantum drop in the magnitude of the war, back to its 1960–1961 level. The GVN, meanwhile, has mounted a massive two-pronged offensive, one military and one persuasional, both psychological. Military pressure on the NLF is intensified through constant sweep operations and other military activities. At the same time the NLF members are being bombarded in the jungles with leaflets, and messages reaching them by other means, offering accommodation ("Liberation Army Men. You have been sold out again. By the Northerners. They've gone home and left you to

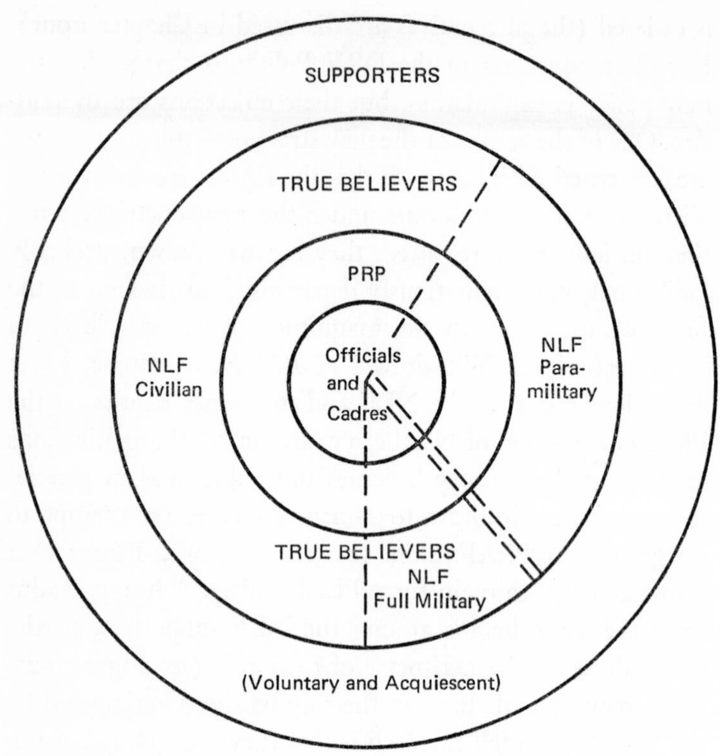

Figure 3-2 Circle: NLF Power Base

hold the sack. Just as they did in 1954. Of course now all hope of winning is gone. However, the *Chieu Hoi* program and *Doan Ket* beckon. Land, jobs, a political life, whatever you want, await you. Leave your hopeless condition without shame and return to the Government side. . . .") The campaign peals off another thick layer of NLF supporters from the circle, and it shrinks once again. Now only the hard core remains, the untouchables at the center of the circle. They number a few thousand. They have no intention of quitting. Some go to North Vietnam. Some retire to the most remote areas of the country to carry on the fight. Conflict is confined to the back country, a politics-with-guns condition. This is not exactly peace, but neither is it war. The rest of the country is reasonably secure. The business of nation building goes forward. Gradually in the back country the insurgency incident rate drops, though even ten years later sporadic guerrilla activity is reported. Meanwhile, in Hanoi, the leadership — perhaps with some new faces in the Politburo — presses forward with whatever new strategy for unification it has adopted. Such is the scenario.

The outcome of two insurgencies — Greece and Malaya — are suggestive of the idea of private accommodation, although neither should be regarded as a Vietnam blueprint. Being no determinist, the author has little faith in the notion of convertibility of idea and method between one counterinsurgency effort and another; insurgencies grow out of peculiar social and political conditions within individual cultures and are not interchangeable. However, parallel patterns exist. The Greek Communists, after military defeat in 1949, gradually returned, under careful controls, to political activity. They re-entered political life, not as members of a party, but incorporated into the theoretically non-Communist Union of the Democratic Left, whose members were and are an important factor in Greek politics. The "crumble" in Malaya — that is, the last years of the Emergency — is even more illustrative for Vietnam.

The Emergency began in Malaya in June 1948 with the announced Malayan Communist Party (MCP) objective of overthrowing British colonial government. Its strategy and tactics were more or less those of orthodox Maoist revolutionary guerrilla war: gradual buildup of the strength to strike increasingly hard military blows; disruption of the economy, especially the mines and rubber plantations; harassment, wearing down, and destruction of the police and the military; engendering of local people's support through a combination of persuasion, ethnic appeals, and terrorism. But it was an essentially military route to power that the MCP pursued. The struggle fluctuated for nearly five years; then in 1951 it began to decline for the British; this trend was reversed with the arrival of General Gerald Templar, and never again were the British in serious trouble. The next three years saw a war of attrition that was significant but unspectacular. The obvious and spectacular progress came in the political sphere. On July 27, 1955, Malaya held its first general elections. Eighty per cent of the registered voters went to the polls and elected, overwhelmingly, an alliance government headed by Tuanku Abdul Rahman.[7] The new Rahman government, cognizant of the basic fact of political life in Malaya—polyglot, multiracial communalism—chose ministers from all three parties of the Alliance (Malayan, Chinese, and Indian). One of Rahman's first acts upon taking office as Chief Minister, late in August 1955, was a series of nationwide radio broadcasts in which he called for independence within four years (that is, agreed-on withdrawal of the British), appointment of a commission to recommend a suitable revision of the constitution in advance of the day of independence and solicitation of ideas and support for the commission, conversion of the federal legislature to a wholly elected body under an arrangement in which all three of the ethnic communities would be properly represented, and a period of amnesty for members of the MCP.[8] Running through his speeches was the theme that a fine new country was to be built in Malaya, which required the support of

[7] Winning 51 of the 52 seats in the Federal Legislative Council.

[8] The essentials of this amnesty were the promise that those who surrendered would not be prosecuted for past terrorist activities (though they would be investigated) and the assurance that those who promised future loyalty to the government would be freed (the remainder to be imprisoned or deported).

all Malayans if it was to work, and that there would be a place for *all Malayans* in the venture. It was a theme of "incorporation." Among those who heard these broadcasts was one Chen Ping, the top Communist leader and head of the MCP. He wrote a letter to Rahman saying that he was interested in discussing this "brave new world" of which Rahman spoke. After some maneuvering, the two met; this was the famed Baling Conference (near the Thai border) on December 28 and 29, 1955. The two men talked almost nonstop all one day, all that night, and all the next day. At the end, Chen Ping told Rahman that he would surrender his forces in return for legal recognition of the Malayan Communist Party and freedom for its members from any investigation or detention; he also agreed to "lay down arms," which apparently did not mean surrender of arms. This must have seriously tempted Rahman, for he needed peace badly and it would have been his with one word. In retrospect, it seems a tribute to Rahman's wisdom that he rejected the equal-status proposal for the MCP, though continuing the amnesty offer. He told Chen Ping that the MCP was outlawed and would remain outlawed,[9] but that he would offer Chen Ping and other members of the MCP an opportunity to return to the Malayan society providing they came as individuals and not as Communist Party members. This was not acceptable to Chen Ping. The conference broke up, and the war went on for three more years. But certainly it was not a failure from Rahman's viewpoint, for it injected a divisive virus into the Communist Party that steadily weakened it. In the next three years the British and the new Malayan government pressed home their newfound advantages against the MCP: a counterinsurgency

[9] And to this day is outlawed.

war of harassment with primary effort on cutting the guerrillas' ties with the civilian populace, and a political appeal campaign offering the individual members of the MCP an honorable, acceptable way out of the war. The campaign gradually depopulated the guerrilla movement. Chen Ping had about 2,500 men at the time of the Baling Conference. Two years later this strength had been cut in half. In 1960 it was about 500.[10] There never were negotiations in Malaya, nor was there any sort of a conference table settlement.

Doan Ket. Vietnam has today a mechanism for ending the war along Malayan Emergency lines, although admittedly it is an infant state. It is called *Doan Ket* or the National Reconciliation Program (NRP). It incorporates an older and less ambitious amnesty program called *Chieu Hoi*; but whereas *Chieu Hoi* seeks to bring insurgents back into the society, the NRP seeks to bring them back into the political decision-making arena.

The *Chieu Hoi*[11] program was begun in 1963 as a policy enunciation, and no more, the ground rules under which the insurgents could stop fighting and return to the government side. It was not intended, under Diem, to be an amnesty program, and nothing was promised the guerrilla, certainly not amnesty. Yet even from the start the program was in effect a "hidden" amnesty program, because the

[10] Its strength in late 1968 was estimated by Malaysian police officials as still being about 500.

[11] Which means "open arms," or as it officially is translated, "return to the just cause." This terminology was a concession to Diem's sensitivities. He and his brother, Ngo Dinh Nhu, considered the proper treatment of insurgents to be extermination; neither would embrace the principle of amnesty, nor would they accept any name for the program that implied forgiveness, exoneration, or amnesty.

officials who administered it in the rural areas, though Diem appointees, did not share Diem's view that all guerrillas were to be treated as heretics; rather they regarded them in more pragmatic terms, as dangerous nuisances who must be forced or persuaded to stop fighting. Gradually the *Chieu Hoi* program broadened, and after Diem the rules for returning became codified and enunciated and a benefit program added. Activity in the *Chieu Hoi* camps throughout South Vietnam today involves chiefly the practical problems of social reintegration (or accommodation), that is, providing medical care, vocational training, clothing, transportation allowances, financial assistance, and so forth.

Doan Ket extends the *Chieu Hoi* concept and concerns itself, not with integration into society, but with political participation, political rights, political opportunities. The *Doan Ket* promulgation proclamation, April 19, 1967, said it was based on three guiding principles:

1. Community . . . Our ties of blood demand we have tolerance rather than hatred. . . . We must bring together the Vietnamese spiritual heritage bequeathed us by our forefathers. . . .
2. Concord . . . Restoring the harmony of the universe developed by our ancestors in great hardship . . . Let all disagreements and difference be expressed not with steel or at the price of spilled blood, but by democratic means in a spirit of peace and harmony.
3. Progress . . . [*Doan Ket*] will help guide us forward in freedom through the social revolution which the Republic now pursues in the name of social justice.

Specifically the proclamation listed as the "rules" of *Doan Ket:*

First, all those who decide to leave the ranks of the Communists and reintegrate in the national community will be warmly welcomed as citizens with full rights of citizenship. All returnees will be protected by the Government, which will also provide them facilities to build a new life. In other words, every citizen who abandons the Communist ranks will enjoy the rights set forth in the Constitution, including the right to have the law protect his freedom, his life, his property, and his honor, the right to vote and to run for office, the right to go back and live with his family, the right to choose his place of residence, and the right to enjoy the national assistance in the pursuit of his profession.

Second, the citizens who rally to the national cause will be employed in accordance with their ability so that every Vietnamese, without distinction, will have the opportunity to contribute positively to the reconstruction and development of the country.

Third, the citizens who rally to the national cause but who have violated the law under Communist coercion or deception, whether they have been convicted or not, will enjoy all the guarantees set forth in the Constitution.[12] The country will be tolerant to the utmost so they have the opportunity to put their ability and determination to serve and redeem themselves.

This policy was reiterated the following year:

President Thieu reaffirmed the policy of his government to resolve the internal problems of all the South Vietnamese people in an amicable, just and peaceful way in accordance with the principle of one man, one vote. He noted his Government had rejected the principles of retaliation and revenge in favor of national reconciliation. He offered full participation in political

[12] GVN policy with respect to treatment of insurgents who might be chargeable for major crimes is taken directly from the Malayan experience. The Malayan amnesty regulations provided that returnees might be tried for major crimes (and, if found guilty, possibly executed); that is, no legal blanket exoneration was offered them. Although the British reserved the right to bring them to trial, as far as the author can determine, they never exercised that right. Not one Communist who returned under the amnesty program was ever executed, though many clearly were guilty of murder and other capital crimes.

activities to all individuals and members of groups who agree to renounce force and to abide by the Constitution of Viet Nam.[13]

During a press conference at the same time in Honolulu, President Thieu was asked about the political candidacy of the NLF member, and he said: "We stated very clearly that anyone who came from the other side and agreed to abandon Communist ideology, to abandon atrocities, and to lay down his weapons and abide by the Vietnamese constitution would have full rights, and can vote, be elected like anyone else."

Back in Saigon, Thieu again reiterated this position for domestic consumption, saying that full political participation was offered all individuals on a one-man, one-vote basis, adding: "As soon as they [NLF] lay down their weapons . . . and abide by the law of the land, they will enjoy the full rights of citizenship."[14]

Doan Ket has integrated a number of former NLF cadres and officials into political positions. The head of the *Chieu Hoi* program itself, virtually at cabinet level, is a man who two years before had the rank in the PLAF Army equivalent to a brigadier general. There are other examples. In practice, implementation of the program is chiefly at the provincial or district level rather than in Saigon. Province chiefs, for example, have the authority to negotiate the return of NLF cadres and other leaders operating in their provinces. Two methods are employed: (1) The province chief hears by

13 Joint communiqué issued July 20, 1968, by Presidents Johnson of the United States and Nguyen Van Thieu of the Republic of Vietnam following their talks in Hawaii.

14 In a Vietnamese television broadcast on August 23, 1968. In the same broadcast he also reiterated an earlier GVN offer of economic and cultural cooperation and relations with the DRV, providing that PAVN be withdrawn.

rumor or intelligence reports that an NLF cadre in his area may be interested in quitting. The province chief contacts a relative of the person in a GVN-controlled village or some other go-between whom both the NLF cadre and the province chief trust, and the return is consummated. (2) The NLF cadre takes the initiative and through some trusted intermediary asks the province chief what he is prepared to offer. At least 50 per cent of those returning under the *Chieu Hoi* program do so under some sort of prearrangement rather than simply walking out of the jungles, hands in the air, waving a safe-conduct pass.

The Southerner in the NLF who is fighting for political power wants that power in order to install certain virtuous conditions, such as justice, economic opportunity, and democracy. His loyalty is not to the NLF as such but to a set of ideals. He does not see his drive for political power in narrow, selfish terms, though he often is ambitious, but as the only way to achieve the good life he seeks. There is no contention between the NLF and the GVN in terms of these ideals. It follows then that the offer of an opportunity of political power can cause him to stop fighting. Such is the assumption of the fledgling *Doan Ket* program: the chance to come back not just into the society but into the political arena. Such also is private accommodation. The process of course is uncertain, and its effectiveness varies greatly from province to province. It may not make much sense to an outsider, but it is an authentic Vietnamese arrangement, quite in harmony with Vietnam's political heritage and style of politics.

In short, then, the prognosis for Vietnam (but not a prediction) is that events can move toward an intensification of violence and end in decisive victory for one side (defeat, of course, for the other side). Or events can move toward a diminution of violence — that is, accommodation — achieved either formally through public and international negotiations, or by "southernization" of the struggle, chiefly with private arrangements among Southern elements of the NLF and the GVN, or by a combination of these two.

CHAPTER FOUR

STRATEGY PAST AND FUTURE

Regardless of the direction that events on the continuum take, military considerations will remain paramount in Vietnam. Decisive Victory, of course, is essentially a military route, but Accommodation also requires great inputs of military effort. Vietnam, after all, is a war. The intent of this chapter is to explore the major strategic options open to the DRV and the NLF, and their limitations. We first consider the three early strategies, two of which have been tried: the Organizational Weapon or *Khoi Nghia* (General Uprising), and Revolutionary Guerrilla War (and its variant, Interim Revolutionary Guerrilla War including the 1967–1968 Winter–Spring Campaign); and one which has never been tried: Coalition Government. Then, after taking note of the politics of the Politburo in Hanoi, we turn to future strategic options: (*a*) Regular Force strategy (or the Quick Victory doctrine); (*b*) Neorevolutionary Guerrilla War; and (*c*) Negotiated Settlement.

Eight-Year Search for a Victory Formula

It is useful to look at the DRV-NLF effort in terms of doctrine. The past eight years have witnessed a never-ending hunt for the right mix of military and political effort that would yield victory, unification for the DRV, and political power for the NLF. From the leaders' view, the problem is not how to survive or how to continue to exist but how to go through the gates of victory. After eight years the successful formula still eludes them. The initial doctrine was *Khoi Nghia* or General Uprising, here termed the Organizational Weapon as being more descriptive; it prevailed from early 1959 through late 1963. Then orthodox Revolutionary Guerrilla War began to dominate strategic thinking. But the tactics and strategy that won against the French proved inadequate, and in mid-1967 orthodox Revolutionary Guerrilla War gave way to a variant form, what is here termed *ad hoc* or Interim Revolutionary Guerrilla War, which includes the 1967–1968 Winter–Spring Campaign. These past and present doctrines are now examined, together with the doctrine of Coalition Government, which has not been tried.

Doctrine seems more important in Communist societies than in open societies, with their thousand-year history of muddling through. Vietnam's Communist history, as well as the world-wide movement, has long debated strategy for insurgencies. Michael Conley,[1] in his excellent historical treatise, defined these as a Left Strategy, a Right Strategy, and a United Front from Below Strategy. The Left Strategy is classic communism. Through agit-prop work the masses' revolutionary fervor rapidly is raised. The Party — unencumbered by entangling alliances and with a minimum of organizational work — engenders social pathology and in the confusion seizes power, literally from the streets. This is the

1 *Building Social Viability in an Insurgent Environment: A Positive Strategy for Displacing Insurgent Infrastructure in South Vietnam* (Washington, D.C.: CRESS American University, scheduled to be published in 1969).

single leap into the saddle maneuver. It is rigid, unbending, deterministic, and romantically unsophisticated, if not simpleminded. It is Che Guevara in Bolivia. As its success rests chiefly on timing, it must peak on the wave of discontent. Guerrilla war contributes to generating social pathology, but the action is in the capital and other centers of incumbent power. Definition of the enemy of Left Strategy is anyone or anything opposing the drive for early seizure of power, the classic "enemy of the people." Right Strategy stands, distinct from the naïve and pure Left Strategy, as somewhat cynical and opportunistic, but more in consonance with the ways of the world. Its essence is political coalition, the popular-front technique. Deals are made. People and organizations are used, betrayed, and discarded. Alliances are formed and sold out and ideals adjusted, daily if necessary, to fit the exigencies of the moment. Yesterday's enemy becomes today's blood brother. The guerrilla is a factor in the equation as a force of occasional utility which can hasten events along by cutting down the power of others, especially in rural areas, through quiet assassinations or other forms of intimidation. The enemy of the Right Strategy is anyone or anything opposing the coalition and its short-run goals. The third route is the United Front from Below Strategy, or in Maoist terminology, the "four-class approach."[2] A shadow

[2] See, especially, Lin Piao, "Long Live the People's War," *Peking Review,* Vol. VIII (September 1965); also in William E. Griffith, *Sino-Soviet Relations, 1964–1965* (Cambridge, Mass.: The M.I.T. Press, 1967). Neo-revolutionary Guerrilla War advocates can interpret Mao doctrine in two ways: (1) rigidly, by holding that Maoism is universal, timeless, and infallible; and, with the general rule, they approach the struggle exactly as the Chinese approached the struggle against the Japanese in the 1930's; (2) flexibly, on the grounds that Maoist people's war today requires modification and adjustment; under the latter interpretation, minor Maoist principles can be corrected but not major ones, such as the idea of a self-reliant, self-supporting protracted conflict.

government, created parallel to the incumbent government, redirects and reorients the civilian population of the country. The parallel structure is independent of the Establishment and is not some sort of collaborative arrangement as in the case of the Right Strategy. The new organizations proselyte the members and raid the leadership of opposition socio-political movements. All organized opposition — whether trade-union, farm cooperative, or local government — is diminished, fragmented, frustrated, compromised, or destroyed. The process necessarily is drawn out into a protracted conflict. In time the *de jure* government is supplanted, and the shadow becomes reality. The enemy is any individual or any group that represents organized opposition, real or potential, even something as harmless as a sports club. While there is no one-to-one relation between this triad of historical strategies and past and present strategies in Vietnam, elements of the debate are clearly visible.

Organizational Weapon. The NLF's original doctrine, *Khoi Nghia* or General Uprising, is a social myth — in the Sorelian sense,[3] traceable back to the proletarian myth of the General Strike. Through creation of social pathology or simple anarchy in the Vietnam countryside, by means of selective terror and motivation of the villager through well-organized struggle movements, the revolutionary consciousness of the villager is raised until that golden moment when the spirit explodes simultaneously in all the villages of the

[3] Georges Sorel, *Reflections on Violence* (New York: Collier Books, 1961). As used here, the term "myth" means not a superstitious or erroneous belief but rather an idea of great moment that guides a person's life. Sorel cited the Christian myth of the Second Coming of Christ as an example of the social myth, noting the great benefits Christianity, in its formative days, derived from the apocalyptic myth that Christ would return to earth, the pagan world would be ruined, and the kingdom of saints would be inaugurated.

country into the General Uprising. The people seize power. *Khoi Nghia* is a combination of sociopsychological activities and terrorism augmented by intensive but low-grade guerrilla warfare. Its mechanism is the Struggle Movement (*dau tranh*), and its specific programs are three: *dan van* (action against the people), *dich van* (action against the enemy), and *binh van* (action against the military); collectively the three *van* add up to political *dau tranh,* the nonmilitary half of the Struggle Movement. The military half, here termed the *violence program,* formally is called armed *dau tranh.*

Political *dau tranh* is the siren call to consecration, putting flesh on the bones of *Khoi Nghia* and converting the someday apocalypse into today's events. *Dau tranh* is composed of commitment, hatred, ambition, grievance, revenge, and aspiration. An ex-NLF cadre told the author: "*Dau tranh* is all-important to a revolutionist. It marks his thinking, his attitudes, his behavior. His life, his revolutionary work, his whole world are *dau tranh.* The essence of his existence is *dau tranh.*" To the true believer in the NLF it explains the unexplainable, adds a new larger-than-life dimension to daily mundane activity. A social myth such as *Khoi Nghia* is vital to the true believer, to catch his imagination, heighten his revolutionary consciousness, rouse him to battle. Without a vision of the sort provided by such a myth there can be no militancy. Whether the myth ever becomes reality is largely irrelevant. What matters is that people act out their lives on the assumption of its truth.

If the General Uprising was the great NLF social myth, the struggle movement was its great social fantasy. For here, with a backdrop of high drama, every man could fling himself into the hero's role. The young crusader could embark on a great quest and look the dragon Authority in the face with courage. To the timid old man, for all his life the Persevering Tortoise, came the moment of destiny when he could say to himself and all the world: "This one thing I do." Cinderella and all the other fools could still believe there was magic in the mature world if one mumbled the secret incantation: solidarity . . . union . . . concord. The meek, at last, were to inherit the earth; riches would be theirs and all in the name of justice and virtue. So out of their thatch-roofed houses they came, pouring through their villages and onto the highways of Vietnam, gullible, misled people, pawns of a vast and abstract power struggle, turning the countryside into a bedlam, toppling one Saigon government after another, confounding the Americans, a sad and awesome spectacle, a mighty force of people, a river the Communists hoped to use and then dam. This was the struggle movement.[4]

Khoi Nghia is a faith, *dau tranh* an attitude, but more than this is required to win power. Shoring up this metaphysical base are the three political action programs: *dan van*, *dich van*, and *binh van*, plus the armed *dau tranh* (or violence program). Every act of the NLF, every statement by its leaders, every decision taken at Central Committee or village committee level has come within the framework of these action programs.

Dan van is an administrative program in the so-called liberated areas, those parts of South Vietnam under NLF sociopolitical control. *Dan van* activities seek to provide material assistance or psychological support for the cause, assure safe haven for the NLF Army, produce food, manufacture or assemble weapons and other instruments war. The liberated areas represent a major source of manpower where recruitment goes on both for the NLF Army and for

[4] Douglas Pike, *Viet Cong* (Cambridge, Mass.: The M.I.T. Press, 1966), p. 92.

its civilian elements. Much of the *dan van* effort seeks to create internal defense structures, known as combat hamlets or fighting hamlets, that is, villages that will try to fend off Vietnamese government forces, usually with the aid of local PLAF units. *Dan van* has many financial tasks: collecting "taxes," selling "war-bonds," and engaging in other fund-raising efforts that are extortion in everything but name. Permeating these activities, but not separated from them, is communication and indoctrination work, carried on by special agit-prop cadres and employing most of the techniques found in Communist societies: emulation campaigns, massive propaganda sessions, *kiem thao* or self-criticism sessions, education (which is indistinguishable from indoctrination in content though differing in organization). Daily mass meetings are held in the villages, addressed by agit-prop cadres. In the evening people are again assembled, and newspaper-reading cells read from NLF newspapers, asking for comments and questions. The unvarying theme is hatred:

> If there was an essence of the NLF indoctrination effort, if there was an *élan vital* that permeated its system, if there was one emotion the leadership found of greater utility than all others combined, if there was any personality trait that differentiated the Vietnamese of the two camps, indeed if one were obliged to write the history of the NLF in a single word, it would be *hate*.[5]

In sum, the leadership regards *dan van* as a source of material support, an indoctrination structure, and a rudimentary future Vietnamese society.

Dich van is the set of nonmilitary activities of the NLF directed against the people living in GVN-controlled areas,

[5] *Ibid.*, pp. 283–284.

both rural and urban; the military activities come under the armed *dau tranh* or violence program. Through the years NLF cadres have demonstrated great imagination and resourcefulness in pursuing various *dich van* activities. Typical are propaganda leaflets surreptitiously placed during the week end in the desks of students in a provincial town school to be found on Monday morning by the students, or cars stopped on the Saigon-Dalat road an hour before dusk one afternoon, the passengers led to a clearing a half mile from the road where they are lectured by an agit-prop cadre. Alternatively, an effigy of the U.S. President may be floated down a river past a district or town market place where it is viewed by thousands of persons in the market. There are also daily broadcasts by Radio Liberation from just above the 17th Parallel, to be heard by Vietnamese who choose to tune in the frequency. An armed propaganda team may appear in a GVN-controlled village some afternoon when the local defense force is off on a mission for the purpose of assembling the villagers and performing a short drama that is part entertainment and part propaganda. Rumors are spread. Local demonstrations by non-NLF townspeople are infiltrated, captured, and turned to NLF purposes. All of these are examples of *dich van*. Another phase of it is seeking support from organizations both inside and outside Vietnam to serve the NLF's ends. For example, the South Vietnam People's Committee for Solidarity with the American People, a member of the NLF, conducts correspondence with American individuals and organizations militantly opposed to American involvement in the Vietnam war.[6]

[6] The NLF carries on extensive activity abroad, usually working in the same building as the DRV representatives, to engender support for its cause. It has representatives in Albania, Algeria, Bulgaria, Cambodia,

The formidable *binh van* program is a proselyting effort among the Vietnamese Armed Forces and the GVN, with the goal of destroying the military and governmental structure by nonmilitary means. The target is the individual soldier or civil servant. Ideally, the *binh van* program would induce universal desertion or defection to the NLF; failing this, it seeks at the very least to lower morale of the soldier or civil servant so he pursues his activities with lessened enthusiasm. *Binh van* techniques include the enunciation and dissemination of the NLF's policy of welcoming all Vietnamese now opposing it to NLF ranks, as well as wide and intensive war of nerves and intimidation, usually against elite ARVN units such as the Rangers or Paratroopers. In addition, undercover agents are employed to penetrate the military and civil service and work from within. Family ties and friendships are used to reach and motivate persons on the other side; tangible and intangible rewards are offered to those who defect or desert. There are massive propaganda campaigns as well.

While the various *van* programs, combined as political *dau tranh,* move forward, the PLAF pursues its armed *dau tranh*, or as it is termed here, the violence program.[7] This is the all-too-familiar guerrilla war; attacks on government installations; the ambush; systematic harassing of villagers, such as rifle fire into a village from a distance, either to coerce or intimidate; sabotage and subversion, such as blowing up gasoline dumps; kidnaping of villagers, especially

Communist China, Cuba, Czechoslovakia, East Germany, France, Hungary, Mongolia, North Korea, Poland, Rumania, Soviet Union, Sweden, and the United Arab Republic.

[7] It would seem that "violence program" is a better term than "armed struggle," since "armed" implies military activity and much of the violence program consists of such activities as kidnapings and assassinations, which are not activities associated with the military.

village leaders; assassinations and executions of individuals. This is terrorism, applied by the NLF judiciously and selectively. Terror, turned on and off, paradoxically produces both pro- and anti-NLF feelings among rural people. It engenders fear and hatred, the first usually predominating; but when terror is relaxed, after an area-wide campaign, an exaggerated sense of relief spreads through the villages. Terror, the NLF believes, is virtually useless against a dedicated opponent. In general, the theoreticians consider terror a weapon of the weak which, as control increases, should be used less. They hold that from terror comes rapid but quickly diminishing returns and that terror is successful only when the objectives of the terrorist have popular support.

Khoi Nghia essentially is a social or organizational route to power rather than a military one. It came perilously close to success in the anarchical situation that developed during and after the last days of the Diem government. The NLF stood at the shore of victory, but slowly the tide ebbed. The reasons are complex, stemming basically from the fact that the NLF no longer held the monopoly of organized opposition to the Diem government. New sociopolitical alignments developed in South Vietnam involving the rise of the Buddhists, students, and South Vietnamese military as political factors (all three previously had been dormant). *Khoi Nghia* as the main route to power was abandoned, though certain of its forms, such as the struggle movement, continued. All the *van* programs, for example, remain active today. But whereas in the 1959–1963 period the ratio between political *dau tranh* and armed *dau tranh* probably was something like 10:1 (in terms of allocation of resources, man-days expended, etc.), by late 1967 the ratio had dropped to something like 2:1, a marked change but still a case in which twice as much effort was being put into political activities as into the violence program.

Revolutionary Guerrilla War. Throughout the war with the French the Viet Minh pursued a strategy borrowed from the Chinese called the Three-Stage Strategy (now described by Hanoi historians as resistance, general offensive, and general uprising). This Revolutionary Guerrilla War, developed by China's Mao Tse-tung, amended and adapted by North Vietnamese Defense Minister General Vo Nguyen Giap, consists of guerrilla activities in a revolutionary context, leading to a full-scale civil war and culminating in a general offensive military campaign by more or less regular military units. It is a military route to power aided by various political activities including *dau tranh.*

This orthodox Revolutionary Guerrilla War, as refined and developed by General Giap in the early 1960's and as practiced by the NLF in South Vietnam, had these characteristics:[8]

1. Doctrinal assertion that by using the judo principle (an enemy's own strength turned against him), a small, poorly equipped military force can defeat a larger, better-equipped one. It does so through the use of an agrarian-based movement that engages in protracted conflict, a war of gradual attrition and slow strangulation, moving from the remote rural areas to capture ultimately the enemy's urban strongholds.

2. Organization that forever seeks the ideal of perfection. Through organization comes mobilization, and through mobilization, motivation. This trinity — organization, mobi-

[8] For a fuller discussion of Revolutionary Guerrilla War see Pike, *op. cit.,* Chapter 2.

lization, and motivation — combine to yield a mystique of warfare. It is said that Napoleon introduced to the world the concept of the modern mass army to serve the nation-state, linked to it by ideology; that he transformed the fighting man from the professional mercenary motivated by money to the civilian conscript motivated by nationalism. Perhaps what General Giap and, before him, Mao Tse-tung have done is to carry Napoleon's concept one step further. Revolutionary Guerrilla War erases the line between civilian and military, as Napoleon erased the line between professional and citizen soldier. Orthodox Revolutionary Guerrilla War, employing both armed and political struggle, progresses according to a set of laws through three stages: defensive (or contention), equilibrium, and finally, general counteroffensive; in the early stages the political struggle dominates, then the military struggle becomes paramount until near the victorious end when there is a return to the political struggle. Mandatory is an ever-rising tempo of combat. Momentum is developed relentlessly but not recklessly.

3. Infinite, meticulous, endless attention to mundane matters of logistics and administration. Moving troops rapidly is one of General Giap's unique abilities, made possible by the careful stockpiling along the route of arms, ammunition, food, and medical supplies often involving unbelievable effort. For example, in 1951 to prepare for the four-day Vinh Yen battle, Giap moved 5,000 tons of rice, ammunition, and other supplies to the battlefield area, requiring *two million man-days of labor*. The late Bernard Fall described Giap's Viet Minh war victories as "logistic victories." This is the point where spirit touches administration.

Study the enemy carefully, never forgetting his peculiar characteristics, never ignoring our own fighting characteristics, always acting on the basis of the Party's military reasoning —

this is the correct scientific way of doing things; this is in accordance with Marxist-Leninist doctrine. Analyze, ponder, conform to the principles of People's war and the reality of the situation—this is the way to win.[9]

4. Deception. There is a high level of deception in Revolutionary Guerrilla War. In fact, some military experts assert deception is its only noteworthy aspect. Warfare in early Vietnam was rampant with deception, and even institutionalized it. The three elements of an ancient Vietnamese army were: the *Chinh Binh* or "real army" (the overt military force); the *Ky Binh* or "hidden army" (covert, fluid, invisible, guerrillalike); and the *Nghi Binh* or "phantom army" (which didn't exist at all but which any good Vietnamese general could make his opponent believe did exist as a means of frightening and disheartening him). Deception in some cases involves hiding the truth not only from your enemy but also from your own forces. In eight years of reading NLF and DRV newspapers, radio broadcast transcripts, and published statements, the author has yet to encounter a single account of a lost battle, a military or political setback, or even casualties. This has great meaning. Perception by the enemy can be, and has been, decisive. The French were exhausted by warfare after Dien Bien Phu, but so were the Viet Minh—exhausted and bankrupt in material resources. As happened in earlier Vietnamese history, however, victory went to the side better able to maintain its appearance of equanimity, the one that most successfully hid its internal difficulties from the world.

Faced with a new enemy and new doctrinal problems, the DRV and NLF theorists hammered Revolutionary Guerrilla

[9] Vo Nguyen Giap, *People's War, People's Army* (New York: Praeger, 1962).

War into a new mold. For a time they were successful. From 1963 to early 1965 the tide of war ran dangerously against the GVN. By February 1965 the GVN had nearly reached the limit of its defenses — ARVN reserve battalions were being decimated one after another in systematic fashion. Once its reserve units were gone, all its installations and the cities, even though defended by troops, would lie exposed and open to attack, for then the enemy could mass his forces without fear of reinforcement for the point under attack. Individual installations could be picked off one by one. At this point, in February 1965, America faced the hard decision of whether to abandon Vietnam or come into the war with ground troops. The latter decision, of course, was the one made. The rest of 1965 and early 1966 saw a gradual receding of the NLF-DRV tide of victory.[10] The techniques of orthodox Revolutionary Guerrilla War began to prove inadequate for General Giap's needs. The war reached equilibrium and then began to move against the DRV. Historians probably will fix as the second major turning point in the war the battle of Ia Drang Valley. DRV commanders ordered some 2,000 troops, elements of the PAVN 66th Regiment into combat against the famed, newly arrived U.S. First Cavalry Division to test the tactics and weaponry of this unique military organization.[11] It was the bloodiest battle of the war to that point, fought for seven bitter days in November down the Ia Drang Valley from Pleime to the Cambodian border. From testimony of prisoners and defectors later, it was learned that probably 1,200 of the 2,000

[10] By this time the DRV was deeply involved with PAVN infantry fighting in South Vietnam. Dispatch of these troops in numbers began in late 1964, and they began arriving in the South in early 1965; at that time the trip took three to four months.

[11] Which, for example, uses an average of 135,000 gallons of gasoline and other petroleum products per day.

men in the PAVN 66th Regiment died or were permanently disabled at Ia Drang. What was worse, from General Giap's standpoint, whole units, platoon-sized and larger, were wiped out to the last man in the experimental attacks against the Americans. The North Vietnamese displayed great courage and skilled use of the tactics they knew but simply could not match the firepower and mobility of the First Cavalry Division.[12] The conclusion forced on the DRV generals by Ia Drang was that the military (but not the political) techniques of orthodox Revolutionary Guerrilla War had been outdated by a generation of military technology. War at one time could be won with crossbows. The tactics that delivered victory in the Viet Minh war, however impressive once, had been relegated by science to the military history textbook.

Interim Revolutionary Guerrilla War. So began a search for new strategy and doctrine. In their effort the DRV generals were obliged to face three major technological problems: the enemy's greater use of long-range weapons, such as naval shelling; his increased use of air power, such as the B-52 plane; and his improved mobility. These are purely military considerations. War, as von Clausewitz stated long ago, consists of two elements: mass and movement. The mass ranged against PAVN and PLAF was superior in terms of both mass of men and mass of firepower. The Allies had greater

[12] Even though most of the Americans in the First Cavalry Division were at the time young, green, and without combat experience. The American Military Advisory Command, Vietnam, announced that First Cavalry Division losses at Ia Drang were 240 killed, 460 wounded. Heaviest U.S. losses came in the first hour of the first day of battle, November 17, when a First Cavalry battalion was ambushed by a 500-man PAVN force.

numbers of men; and they had greater firepower, sheer ability to throw lead. American First Cavalry troops going into battle carried 500 rounds of ammunition, while PLAF troops carried 30 to 50 rounds. Behind the infantry was the recoilless rifle, the artillery, the air strike, the B-52 raid. The Americans also had the advantage in movement, through the mobility provided by the ubiquitous helicopter, which revolutionized warfare in Vietnam. Allied mobility permitted the sudden arrival of troops in an area previously valuable to the PLAF because of its inaccessibility. It also permitted the phenomenon of "doubling-up" of troops. The author talked to one U.S. Marine captain who, by accident, fought in three skirmishes in three provinces between the rising and setting of one sun — he had been "tripled" by the helicopter.

As a search for a workable doctrine went on, the Americans built up their forces, from 23,000 men in February of 1965 to some 450,000 two years later. The DRV leaders strove to match the buildup, with respect to both men and firepower. Troops went down the Ho Chi Minh trail as fast as conditions permitted; the trail itself was widened and improved so that eventually the entire trip could be made by vehicle, eleven days from Hanoi to outside Kontum. Firepower was increased with the introduction of new Communist-nation weapons. PAVN and the PLAF soon were fighting with B-40 barrage rockets, artillery, antiaircraft guns, flame throwers, occasional tanks, and a whole family of automatic weapons. The image of the PLAF soldier as a barefoot farmer fighting with only a homemade shotgun was as fanciful as the view that American planes bombed a North Vietnam lying helpless like Ethiopia in 1938 (the air defenses of North Vietnam are the most advanced and sophisticated the world has ever seen in action in wartime, infinitely superior to the air defenses of Berlin, Tokyo, or London in World War II). PAVN and the PLAF received adequate quantities of the best military equipment that the Communist world could produce.

The chief problem remained, however, and it was not logistical but doctrinal. By mid-1967 the bankruptcy of orthodox Revolutionary Guerrilla War was obvious even to the rank and file. The DRV-NLF forces had not won a single battle of significance in two years. Allied firepower was eating deeply into their reserves of men and supplies. In the same two-year period the PLAF desertion rate had doubled every six months. More and more troops were required from the North, and much to the Northern generals' displeasure, the war steadily was shifting to PAVN shoulders (by late 1968, some 75 per cent of the daily combat in South Vietnam was being carried by PAVN). Logistics, always a bottomless well, became a nightmare as supplies were steadily discovered and destroyed. Morale sagged, especially among the PLAF troops. The NLF village structure was in disarray, the NLF financial system under great stress. Most serious of all, true believers were asking openly whether the dogmas of the past were adequate for the stormy present. A loss of ideological faith was leading to confusion and demoralization among the key figures in the South, the cadres. Dissension in the Politburo arose over the lack of progress and particularly over General Giap's "no win" policy. A sense of impotence developed among Northern leaders as American planes continued to pound away at North Vietnamese transportation and communication centers, curtailing the flow of food, consumer goods, and people throughout the country, as well as war matériel in from China and out to South Vietnam. From the Communist capitals abroad, especially from Peking but also from Moscow, came muted but stronger criticism of the means by which the leadership was conducting the war.

All of this, of course, was painfully apparent to the Politburo members, whose hands by now fully controlled the war reins. The moment of decision, the point at which it was clear things no longer could go on as they had, came in the summer of 1967. In Saigon that summer there were many indications that a basic change in Hanoi's strategy was in the offing. Many experts in Saigon predicted a return to pure "protracted conflict" guerrilla war. What came, however, was not a slowdown but an acceleration of the war's tempo. The press came to label this new strategy the Go-for-Broke doctrine. It is here termed Interim or *ad hoc* Revolutionary Guerrilla War since it seeks to preserve the conceptual framework of orthodox Revolutionary Guerrilla War but contains a host of new concepts such as intensive urban attacks. It clearly bears the stamp of General Giap[13] with regard to concept, execution, timing, shifting of forces, handling of logistics. Considerable evidence, all of it inferential, indicates that General Giap sold his new strategy to the Politburo as a single campaign that would be militarily decisive. For the Politburo, in all probability, it was the "least worst" of the options open at the moment.

A great deal is known about this Interim or *ad hoc* Revolutionary Guerrilla War from captured documents and the testimony of prisoners and defectors. Also, a surprising amount of our knowledge comes from General Giap's public explanations, particularly his book *Big Victory, Great Task*.[14]

[13] Some observers maintain that the new strategy's 1967-1968 Winter-Spring campaign was not willingly Giap's but was forced on him against his better judgment. Voluntarily or not, clearly it bore his hallmark. Quite possibly the campaign owed much to the thinking of Le Duan.

[14] Vo Nguyen Giap, *Big Victory, Great Task* (New York: Praeger, 1967).

Victory — that is, unification of Vietnam — comes by military action in South Vietnam, General Giap maintains. It does not come through negotiations; in his book he dismisses the idea by never mentioning it. Nor, he says, is victory achieved through U.S. elections. The only way to win, he repeats to the point of tedium, is *militarily, on the ground, in South Vietnam*. This, of course, is the Giap thesis, one not shared by all members of his Politburo. The specific blueprint of his strategy was called the Winter–Spring Campaign.

The Winter–Spring Campaign of 1967–1968. The campaign was divided into three phases. Phase I came in October, November, and December of 1967 and entailed "coordinated fighting methods," that is, fairly large, set-piece battles against important fixed installations or enemy concentrations. The battles of Loc Ninh in Binh Long Province, Dak To in Kontum Province, and Con Thien in Quang Ngai Province, all three in the mountainous interior of South Vietnam along the Cambodian and Laotian borders, were typical and, in fact, major elements of Phase I. These battles resulted in heavy DRV casualties — General Giap lost 5,000 men killed or permanently injured at Dak To — but probably he judged that Phase I was inconclusive. The first phase did serve to increase the grumblings of certain of the so-called professional (that is, nonpolitical) generals in Hanoi, line commanders who complained they had lost sizable numbers of good men in these mountain battles to no purpose, in a campaign large enough to extract a real price but too small to be decisive.

Phase II came in January, February, and March of 1968 and involved great use of General Giap's "independent fighting methods," that is, large numbers of attacks by fairly small units, simultaneously, over a vast geographic area and using the most refined and advanced techniques of guerrilla war. Whereas Phase I was fought chiefly with PAVN troops (at that time some 55,000 were in the South), Phase II was fought mainly with PLAF troops. The crescendo of Phase II was the lunar new year or Tet offensive, begun in the middle of a truce on January 30, in which 70,000 troops attacked 32 of South Vietnam's largest population centers. The Tet offensive concentrated on the major cities, on airfields and anything else having to do with aviation, on GVN-Allied logistic, transportation, and communication networks, and on all major headquarters, civilian or military. An analysis of the pattern of attacks indicates that General Giap anticipated, or hoped, that the Tet offensive would have the following effects: (*a*) The Vietnamese Armed Forces, so often described as the "army that won't fight," would not fight and further would disintegrate as a coherent military organization. This did not happen. The Vietnamese Army stood and fought as it never had before; this was its finest hour. (*b*) The civilian population in South Vietnam would rise up, if not in the *Khoi Nghia,* at least with massive support for the NLF as it battered its way into the cities. Neither did this happen. There was no General Uprising, and it now seems naïve that the leadership should have expected it. There was not even the proffering of public support that might have been expected. In this, Giap probably was the victim of overoptimistic reporting by his people in the South who had reported a rising tide of anti-Americanism. This feeling did exist to a certain degree, but it was not as great as Giap's cadres in the South interpreted. A worse mistake on their part was to equate anti-Americanism with pro–Viet Congism. (*c*) The American participation in the war could through judicious blows be momentarily halted or shunted aside. Giap saw as the great

American military strength in Vietnam, not its troops, but its communication-command-response structure, that is, its ability to communicate information on attacks in remote areas rapidly to headquarters, where a command decision can quickly be made and a coordinated response ordered, the dispatch of heliborne troops, air strikes, and so forth. Giap seems to consider this American mechanism like a fine watch, beautifully constructed but very sensitive and easily stopped. Tet offensive attacks were launched not on American troop units — in fact, they were ignored — but on American communication centers, headquarters and above all on American air installations. This also was a failure. The mechanism was not as delicate as anticipated.

Phase III, in April, May, and June of 1968, originally was to have combined the independent and coordinated fighting methods, culminating in a great fixed battle somewhere. This was what captured documents guardedly referred to as the "second wave" (in Saigon known as the "other shoe," or the "Dien Bien Phu gambit"). Possibly it was to have been Khe Sanh, the U.S. Marine base in the far northern corner of Vietnam; or the old imperial capital of Hué; or Saigon itself. There was no second wave, chiefly because events in Phases I and II did not develop as expected; the Winter–Spring Campaign did not, as they say in the theater, build. Still, during Phase III the war reached its bloodiest tempo in eight years. American losses during the three months averaged nearly 500 killed per week; the GVN losses were double that rate; and the PAVN-PLAF losses were nearly eight times the American loss rate. In the Winter–Spring Campaign, Giap began with about 195,000 PLAF main force and PAVN troops. During the nine months he lost (killed or permanently disabled) about 85,000 men. During the same period at least 60,000 men and perhaps more came down the Ho Chi Minh trail from North Vietnam as replacements.

The Winter–Spring Campaign was military, but there was a nonmilitary dimension to it, both internally, in South Vietnam, and internationally. In South Vietnam, especially in Phase III, came a stepped-up program of terrorism, particularly against the GVN pacification program. There were increased organizational and motivational work by political cadres and greater effort in the three *van* programs, especially the deadly *binh van* or proselyting program. Captured documents and prisoner reports indicate that the leadership counted heavily on ARVN troops not only refusing to fight but openly joining the NLF en masse. Paper organizations (noted in Chapter One) were created for the purpose of quickly employing their services. Collectively these were known as the Patriotic Armed Forces, which for a period billed itself as the armed force of the Alliance. *Dich van* efforts were also intensified, and a great effort was launched to engender NLF support in the cities. It is a safe estimate that for every five PLAF soldiers in the offensive there was one political cadre in action. During individual city operations in early February political cadres moved from house to house or among the early morning crowds, mingling with the people, explaining the General Uprising and soliciting support. Many carried with them lists of names of persons ostensibly willing to take part in public demonstrations. A common theme used by these cadres was that the NLF stood for democracy, social welfare, neutralism, and peace. Commando units striking at specific targets in the cities had satellite political cadres circling, four or five blocks away, the installation under attack, keeping people out of the fire fight and soliciting support. A special "Coalition" flag was flown. In the villages cadres were describing the new "revolutionary administration" as a *dan van* activity; this was portrayed as a replacement of the GVN authority at the village level with "people's revolutionary state power." Many of these activities were not important. What is important is to note the enormous effort — especially in vitally needed manpower — expended in the political or nonmilitary aspect of the Winter–Spring Campaign.

Meanwhile, abroad, DRV diplomats were weaving a "talks" campaign into a fabric of many threads, one which was greatly intensified after the Tet offensive with its drastic effect on official thinking and public sentiment in virtually every country of the globe. Originally the Hanoi "talks" overture was designed to enhance the Hanoi peace image, divide its enemy, possibly achieve a halt of air strikes into North Vietnam, reduce Politburo grumbling, and, if the military campaign was successful, help close the victory ring. Hanoi policy with respect to "talks" did not change with or during the Winter–Spring Campaign. What Foreign Minister Nguyen Duy Trinh was saying in May 1968 about meeting the Americans was what he had been saying in December of 1967; in fact he had been making allusions to the possibility of talks as early as February 1967.

In the broadest terms the grand strategy of the Winter–Spring Campaign went beyond General Giap's military contributions. It was a two-salient pincer movement, one military and the other diplomatic or negotiational. Taken together, it was the familiar fighting-negotiating technique that formed the pattern in 1954 at the end of the Viet Minh war, and in Korea prior to and during the armistice talks that ended Korean hostilities. The diplomatic-negotiational salient, in turn, had two prongs. The first was the negotiational ploy, implying the possibility of a political settlement of the war. The second prong of the salient was aimed at the GVN, in the form of the Alliance, which implied the possibility of some arrangement in South Vietnam that would be politically acceptable to the South Vietnamese.

The Winter–Spring Campaign officially ended on July 1, 1968. But the military techniques and certain of the political gestures continued, part of the never-ending search for a winning doctrine. But by the end of the Winter–Spring Campaign it was obvious to anyone close to the scene that interim Revolutionary Guerrilla War was as great a failure as its predecessor.

Coalition Government. The third strategy of the past, never tried, is Coalition Government. Whereas *Khoi Nghia* or the General Uprising thesis basically is social, and Revolutionary Guerrilla War in any of its various forms is military, Coalition Government is not political, as might be assumed, but diplomatic. It is not the same as political settlement. Nor is it power-sharing, which is what the term means in Europe (see Chapter Three). As the term was used by the NLF theoreticians who espoused it from the earliest days (and they always were in the minority), Coalition Government is a technique for coming to power; it is not an arrangement but a means. Theoretically it could be used in any country in the world. The scenario, as envisioned by the early NLF advocates, would go something like this:

An elite band of insurgents, beginning in a remote part of the country, launch a political and armed *dau tranh,* shored up if necessary by a social myth such as *Khoi Nghia.* The chief effort is to organize the peoples of that remote area into manageable units. Farmers, women, youth, students, and anyone else available are persuaded or coerced into joining an appropriate group. Eventually, this organized structure comes to total, say, 10 per cent of the population. Then a political claim is staked out. The incumbent government and the world are informed that the new force exists, represents 10 per cent of the population, and therefore deserves — and demands — 10 per cent of the political decision-making power. It appeals to the world's sense of justice and fair play. The group warns that it will continue fomenting social pathology until its demands are met. Turmoil spreads until the world concludes that peace can return only if the insurgents are brought into the decision-making arena. The incumbent government is so counseled by outside powers. It refuses. The pressure grows. Finally the government gives in and hands the insurgent leaders a few cabinet posts (ideally, the Ministries of Information and Rural Affairs). Once inside, the leaders use their new positions to extend their influence, not by means of a palace *coup d'état,* but openly, by employing prerogatives and advantages that those in power normally enjoy. Gradually the new force broadens its base of support, winning over more followers at the grass roots and perhaps even some of the old incumbent groups in the capital. Finally comes a decisive move, "consolidating" power. Victory is achieved.

The heart of the technique is to generate such external pressures on the incumbent government as to require it to share power with the insurgents and then, when inside, by infiltration and superior organizational work at the grass roots — all legitimate perhaps — gradually to take over the reins of government. The success of the strategy rests on the assumption that the incumbent political forces — since they are urban, elitist, nonegalitarian organizations (as usually is the case in developing nations) — cannot or will not imitate the techniques of the challenger, even when fully aware of the danger of losing power because of those techniques. Further, its advocates argue, the method effectively bypasses foreign intervention since what is going on appears to be almost totally a matter of internal politics, and since there is no decisive or dramatic moment to arouse the world until the very end. Although never tested—possibly an example was the near take-over by the Communists in Indonesia—it appears that the Coalition Government strategy would have little prospect of success in a developed society, but it might be effective in an underdeveloped society in Africa or South America.

Strategic Options and Limitations

The question posed—around which revolves the DRV and NLF theoreticians' debate—is this: To achieve unification, ought we to pursue an essentially military route, and if so, should this be a quick victory effort or a protracted conflict; or should we pursue essentially a nonmilitary or political route?

Politics of the North Vietnamese Politburo. The war has a political dimension in Hanoi just as it has elsewhere. Admittedly, it is not as apparent. The world's information on the meaning and the working out of the war in North Vietnam is scandalously inadequate. Being able to work in the dark—while the white glare of the press plays mercilessly on its open-society opposition—has been of inestimable value. The brief references in this chapter to the politics of the Lao Dong Politburo in Hanoi are limited to doctrinal disputes; even so, this description is a mosaic of only scattered pieces, at best tentative and suggestive.

In recent years it was fashionable among scholars to divide

the Politburo members into hard-soft factions, the dogmatists or pro-Chinese faction versus the moderate or pro-Soviet faction, with a smaller faction called the semiopportunists or nationalists-*cum*-Communists standing between. In somewhat simplified terms, Hanoi was seen as a debating forum for arguing the merits of furthering communism by means of wars of liberation versus the method of peaceful coexistence. Onto this was grafted the local debate of how best to achieve unification of North and South Vietnam. The Politburo then could be divided into the pro-Soviet or dove camp and the pro-Chinese or hawk camp. Truong Chinh, the militant and bold revolutionist, stood for battle, alongside the Chinese. General Giap, the more cautious, sided with the Russians against this military adventurism. Nguyen Chi Thanh sided with the Chinese and liberation. So did the Southerners in the NLF Central Committee. Phan Van Dong could be labeled pro-Soviet since he was hesitant about open war, the same role ascribed to Ho Chi Minh unless the expert saw him as a "swing" force, a balance wheel. Recently, however, Vietnam scholars came to regard this division — especially with respect to the Sino-Soviet dispute — as no longer meaningful. As the war continued in South Vietnam and the lessons of combat were driven home, it became apparent that the old categories no longer fit. In fact, the roles reversed. General Giap became the bold leader pressing for quick victory before time ran out, while Truong Chinh, his ancient rival, argued for protracted conflict, that is, a lower-level drawn-out war. The Chinese also calmly switched signals. They who had been advocating ultra-militancy in liberating the South began urging restraint and patience.

We do know that factionalism exists in the Politburo. We also know that all members first and foremost are pro-Vietnamese whose Politburo is remarkable for its stability, continuity, and lack of purges compared with other Communist regimes. Factionalism should not be exaggerated. There is no difference of opinion so far as is known on the objective of unification. The disagreements—and evidence of these appears candidly in public speeches and writings—are over the means of achieving unification.

Politics, as well as history, thus hedge in the theoreticians and form a firm wall of limitation, as will be apparent in the consideration later of the three basic options open to the Politburo: Regular Force strategy, Neorevolutionary Guerrilla War strategy, and Negotiated Settlement strategy. The Winter–Spring Campaign of 1967–1968, which essentially was the child of the Regular Force strategists, clearly involved elements of the other two strategies and quite obviously was a compromise at the Politburo level. It contained a little of something for everyone: big-unit war, guerrilla war, united-front gestures of coalition government, and intimations of a conference table settlement. The political pulling and hauling in the Politburo, illustrated by the Winter–Spring Campaign, can be counted on as a constant in the equation and if the composition of the Politburo changes appreciably, it can become the dominant factor.

Regular Force Strategy. This doctrine has formed the operational code for the conduct of the war to date. It is espoused by General Vo Nguyen Giap, General Van Tien Dung, Prime Minister Phan Van Dong, President Ho Chi Minh, and Le Duan. This group believes that victory is to be attained by the use of more or less regular military force in South Vietnam, applied as quickly as possible. In the allocation of resources it assigns top priority to weaponry and to logistic needs. The maximum number of troops possible is fielded. Tactics involve sudden and massive onslaughts—what General Giap calls the comprehensive and continuous offensive. Its proponents believe that no longer is time on their side, because the enemy has an unmatchable advantage in any long grind-down war of attrition: he is bigger, richer, more numerous. Hence, the proper strategy is to press for a quick decision. This group has been described as advocating Go-for-Broke tactics; perhaps that term overstates the case, but what is sought is the quickest victory possible. Apparently the Lao Dong Central Committee has collectively endorsed the doctrine. Party Resolution 13, approved in April 1967, urges seeking "a decisive victory in South Vietnam in the shortest possible time." This is interpreted by Britain's P. J. Honey, an authoritative scholar of North Vietnam, as a complete and total rejection of the earlier strategy of Protracted Conflict (which is the heart of orthodox Revolutionary Guerrilla War); Honey lists Le Duan, General Nguyen Van Vinh, and the late General Nguyen Chi Thanh, as major proponents of the Regular Force strategy.[15] This doctrine has the backing of the most powerful members of the Politburo. The chief problem faced by General Giap, as leading doctrinaire, is temporal—time that he simply does not have. The logic of his thinking has led him to try to compress events within time, as best exemplified by the launching of the Tet offensive attacks on the cities, despite long-standing advice to win the rural areas, after which "the cities will drop like ripe plums." At Tet there was a dispersion of forces (in all some 200 separate attacks in the first 48 hours of the Tet offensive) rather than the more orthodox concentration of forces. Troops were expended with

[15] See P. J. Honey, "The Offensive: Hanoi's Change of Strategy," *China News Analysis,* March 22, 1968.

an astonishing lavishness, unlike the previous careful husbanding of resources. Logistics failures were common (PAVN ran out of artillery ammunition at Khe Sanh), and there was a consistent failure by top leaders to double-check intelligence reports. Above all, there was great haste, a headlong plunge that differed from previous DRV military behavior in South Vietnam. But this is the way to fight in order to gain quick victory. In striving to meet military and psychological requirements and maintain momentum in the war, General Giap ordered that the enemy be matched in mass and movement, and that the PAVN-PLAF system be charged with new psychic energy.

Regular Force strategy required that the enemy's build-up in weaponry be matched, that is, in a logistics war: the Communist-made AK-47 as the basic infantry weapon of the PLAF versus the U.S.-made M-16 rifle; the Soviet-made RPD machine gun (7.62-mm) versus the U.S.-made M-60 machine gun; the RPG-2 and RPG-7 grenade launchers, both Soviet-made, versus the U.S. M-79 launcher; the Chinese-made 107-mm and the Soviet-made 122-mm and 140-mm rockets, as well as the Soviet-made 152-mm artillery pieces, versus American-made artillery, although seldom did artillery duels take place. The PLAF-PAVN was not able to match the U.S.-Allied-ARVN firepower, but by early 1968 it was able to match or exceed the firepower of the South Vietnamese paramilitary forces, the Regional Force and Popular Force troops.

Regular Force strategy also requires an enormous indoctrination effort among true believers in the South. Vietnamese Communists long have exhibited great faith in the indoctrination process. Programs are based on the assumption that if a Vietnamese is lectured intensively for several weeks, he will be left effectively and permanently with a high *élan* and great faith in the cause. This belief is strangely naïve, quite inconsistent with the mental set and behavioral pattern of the average Vietnamese; moreover, it must be an endless source of disappointment to the individual agit-prop cadre. Relentlessly, the "maturation process" (*truong thanh*) goes on among civilian villagers under NLF control and in the armed forces. Special classes, indoctrination courses, and retraining sessions are held repeatedly in the remote areas of the South for cadres, NLF and PRP members, and other key figures. Deserters, when captured, are sent to special regional-level camps for reindoctrination. Emulation movements and other socialist competition campaigns are staged in NLF-controlled villages. The indoctrination deals with such topics as the substantive nature of the struggle, organizational principles, and specific military or political techniques. The heart of the effort is the generating of hate. At the huge North Vietnamese infiltration camp of Xuan Mai, a special course is required of all trainees; it is called the Hate America Session — three one-hour lectures a week for three months on the subject. Emulation campaigns in the South are also built on hatred; farmers are urged to grow more rice out of hatred for the "invader." A common PLAF slogan is "Live Nobly, Die Gloriously." The purpose of this sort of indoctrination, especially among the PLAF, obviously is an effort to offset the enemy's advantage in firepower and manpower.

Regular Force strategy has assumed these characteristics:

¶ It is more military and less political than earlier strategies. There is superficial deference to the "political struggle" and indeed some effort here, but the main thrust is military: "The military struggle is becoming even more important in playing the decisive role in defeating the enemy on the battlefield."[16] In other words, the military struggle must dominate.

¶ It involves "coordinated fighting methods" (*hop dong cach danh*). This is the task of PAVN troops in the South and the PLAF main force units, and it is explained thus:

> Coordinated fighting methods involve applying the universal principle of concentrating forces to annihilate the enemy. The method is one in which infantry troops constitute the main element. They operate in coordination with other armed branches. They have the capacity to annihilate major units or command posts of the enemy. Coordinated fighting does not depend on the availability of units from all armed branches. Coordinated fighting combines many fighting methods, tactical forms, and tricks of the people's war. It also involves coordination between artillery units and crack special units, between engineer and antiaircraft units, etc. This method puts special emphasis on high efficiency of all kinds of weapons and equipment.[17]

This was the battles of Dak To, Con Thinh, and Loc Ninh. It might have been those of Khe Sanh or the "second wave."

¶ It involves "independent fighting methods" (*doc lap cach danh*), described as follows:

> . . . the principle of using a small number of troops to defeat a large number of troops who possess modern equipment . . . a unique creation of people's war in the South. The common characteristics of this method are: a spirit of positively attacking and annihilating the enemy, developing a high degree of fighting ability, and developing initiative in the armed forces and the people. This method has inflicted heavy losses and rendered the enemy panic-stricken. Some independent fighting is done by crack special units. No matter where the enemy troops are located, and no matter how adequately protected they may be, whether air bases, logistical facilities, U.S. officers' quarters, etc.,

[16] Giap, *Big Victory, Great Task*, p. 54.
[17] *Ibid.*, pp. 66–71.

the Liberation Army's crack special units have been able to harm them seriously. They have dealt vigorous surprise blows at the enemy and rendered him incapable of reacting to them. They have paralyzed the enemy's communications, cut important strategic routes, destroyed military bridges, attacked enemy mechanized vehicles, etc. With independent fighting methods the Liberation Army's antiaircraft units have inflicted considerable losses on the enemy's air force and have restricted his aircraft, especially his helicopters. We use a small force against a larger force, along with a large force to strike at a smaller force. Naturally when a small force fights a large force, [it] must have the following conditions: the quality of units must be high; the targets must be carefully chosen; opportunities must be created and the situation maintained, especially in the face of enemy flaws; and actions must be unexpected and swift.[18]

This was the strategy of the 1968 Tet offensive, when some 70,000 PLAF troops attacked 32 of South Vietnam's largest population centers in a single night. Also, it is the standing instructions to the guerrilla in the South who is to fight alone, on his own; his role is harassing enemy communication lines, hit-and-run raiding of outposts and camps with the objective of forcing the enemy to disperse his forces, performing liaison and supply work for the Main Force units, cutting towns off as much as possible from the countryside to provide a first-echelon defense against counterattacks and military operations in the countryside.

¶ Putting these two methods together creates the "comprehensive offensive." It means

. . . attacking comprehensively and continuously, gaining initiative by attacking the enemy everywhere with all forces and weapons and with all appropriate methods. The comprehensive offensive is a coordinated military and political offensive against the United States and puppet troops and administration, in the mountains, jungle areas, delta, and the cities. It requires great

[18] *Ibid.*, pp. 68–71.

determination, flexibility, and creative military methods. This strategy accumulates great strength for us as it develops from the rural areas to the cities, from the mountains and jungle areas to the delta, the areas regarded by the enemy as indestructible. New prospects and capabilities for offensive strategy are offered, and a comprehensive and continuous offensive is developed of immeasurable and invincible strength.[19]

This is what the Australian journalist Denis Warner has termed the Dien Bien Phu gambit, that is, wide-ranging attacks on a host of positions while slowly and carefully preparing for the major battle somewhere.

¶ Negotiations with the enemy are to be tolerated only if they contribute somehow to diminishing any of the enemy's various military advantages. Possibly there exists a division within the Regular Force strategy camp between the political generals and the so-called "professional" generals, between those who argue in favor of fighting-negotiating and those who advocate a "pure" military approach.

In establishing a doctrine this group seeks to build on past strategies and past doctrinal thinking rather than to break with them. Although Giap indicates little faith in traditional guerrilla war and its mystical protracted conflict, he pays due obeisance. He is too much of a military man to believe he could win a "fifty-year war" with the United States, but protracted conflict and guerrilla war in general comprise such a holy article of faith that all doctrine must appear to harmonize with them. The Regular Force strategy group does not challenge these ideas but uses them, embraces them, and turns them to their advantage.

Despite superficial appearances the Regular Force strategy contains a high element of irrationality, which is the point where logic touches ego. Its chief supporters in the Politburo

19 *Ibid.*, pp. 60–61.

are the old-line ideologues, and its chief if silent opponents are the younger, more pragmatic elements. For Ho Chi Minh and other old ideologues, some of whom have been trying to create a single Communist Vietnam state since 1918, the objective of unification no longer is simply a governmental policy. It is a spiritual crusade. Ho Chi Minh's speeches are the language of a zealot on the subject of unification,[20] and he seems totally hostile to those, inside or outside Hanoi, who advocate any proposal for unification that requires time, that is, a decade or a generation. Ho Chi Minh wants to culminate his life with unification. He wants it now, not when he is gone. It is chiefly this ego involvement of Ho Chi Minh and the top DRV leaders that caused them to cling to the Regular Force strategy in the face of obvious evidence that it was failing.

Neorevolutionary Guerrilla War. Standing in opposition to Regular Force strategy, espoused by General Giap, is Neorevolutionary Guerrilla War strategy, with its chief spokesman General Giap's old political enemy, Truong Chinh. This strategy might also be called "fourth generation" Revolutionary Guerrilla War (the first three being the Chinese Revolution, the Viet Minh war, and the early NLF effort); or the Protracted Conflict thesis. The chief distinguishing characteristic between the two is temporal, the

[20] For example, "Our compatriots in the Southern area are citizens of Vietnam. Rivers can dry up and mountains wear away but this truth stands" (May 3, 1946). "Each day the Fatherland remains disunited, each day you [in the South] suffer, food is without taste, sleep brings no rest. I solemnly promise you . . . the Southern land will return to the bosom of the Fatherland" (October 23, 1956). "South Vietnam is our flesh and blood. . . . Vietnam is one country. South and North are the same family, and no reactionary force can partition it" (September 2, 1957). "Every hour, every minute the people of the North think of their compatriots in the South . . . the Brass Citadel of the Fatherland . . ." (May 9, 1963).

question being: For whom does time work? General Giap argues that time works against the DRV, that as the days pass, the enemy's firepower eats deeper and deeper into his reserves of men and supplies, that he cannot win in the long run but he can win in the short run by mounting a "continuous comprehensive offensive." Truong Chinh takes the opposite stand. He argues that time is the one thing that is on the DRV side, that it is impossible to slug it out with the Americans on a toe-to-toe basis but that the Americans can be defeated by outlasting, outwaiting, outenduring them. Truong Chinh has written extensively on the matter of time and the protracted conflict:

> Time works for us. Time will be our best strategist. . . . The guiding principle of the strategy of our whole resistance must be to prolong the war. To protract the war is the key to victory. . . . In short if we prolong the war thanks to our efforts our forces will grow stronger, the enemy forces will be weakened. . . . To achieve these results the war must be prolonged and we must have time. . . . Those who want "lightening resistance war and rapid victory," who want to bring the whole of our forces to the battle-front to win speedy victory and rapidly to decide the outcome of the war, do not profit from the invaluable experiences of history; indeed they understand nothing of the strategy necessary to our people in this resistance war. . . . All they would achieve would be the premature sacrifice of the bulk of forces in a few adventurous battles; they would commit heroic but useless suicide.[21]

Neorevolutionary Guerrilla War resembles Chinese Communist people's war in many ways: it seeks to exploit contradictions in the imperialist and feudalist camp; it employs the national salvation theme; it uses fully the united-front concept; and it seeks to protect the rural base at all costs.

21 Truong Chinh, *Primer For Revolt* (a facsimile edition of *The August Revolution* and *The Resistance Will Win*) (New York: Praeger, 1963), pp. 112–113. The original works were written in 1946 and 1947.

However, it does not root the struggle to the village in quite the same way as would the Chinese. Nor does it endorse totally the Chinese idea that the struggle must be completely self-reliant and without outside assistance and support; it seems impossible to advocate that the struggle in South Vietnam be conducted without any outside, including North Vietnamese, assistance. Nevertheless it does support the Chinese idea of self-reliance in the sense of a people's war. In fact, one fundamental difference between Regular Force strategy and Neorevolutionary Guerrilla War strategy relates to the question of people versus weapons. The latter strategy makes great use of the notion, from the Chinese, of the superiority of human strength over material strength, the "people as a spiritual atom-bomb." Truong Chinh has declared:

> The decisive factor in any war is the human factor and the revolutionary spirit of man. It is not weapons, not even the modern war materials . . . [or] sound Party leadership [guided by] proper political and military policy lines. . . . It is the bravery of man, not steel and weapons, that decides the outcome of war. . . . The people's war is a powerful weapon.

The Neorevolutionary strategists, who have at least the moral support of the Chinese Communists, believe that the war must be held to a more tolerable level, that the maximum strike effort pays an unnecessarily high price for victory, even assuming it achieves victory. This group believes that the way to meet the enemy's advantages of mass and movement is to go back to Second-Stage guerrilla war, with the plan to *fight and win at Stage Two and never go on to Stage Three*. Under the orthodox Revolutionary Guerrilla War of Mao Tse-tung, it is permissible to shuttle back and forth among the stages, but it is a sharp break with Maoism to believe that victory can be won at Stage Two.

This doctrine, from the DRV standpoint, does have a number of recommendations: it lowers the military profile; there are fewer risks, no large battles lost since none is fought; casualties are held down. With the gnat-swarm type of attack the enemy cannot bring to bear his massive firepower or his vaunted mobility. (What advantage is there in great strength or speed when one is attacked by a swarm of mosquitoes?) By having small-unit attacks, everywhere and continuously, the enemy, one hopes, will be pinned down, constantly occupied, and thus denied initiative.

In broad outline the characteristics of Neorevolutionary Guerrilla War appear to be these:

¶ The Maoist three-stage guerrilla war concept serves as a base but is greatly modified and amended. The major change is the plan to fight and win at Stage Two, never to go on to Stage Three. Specifically, this means more attacks by smaller-sized units. Fewer risks mean fewer casualties; the result is less strain on the system, hence fewer defections and desertions.

¶ The military organizational concept of two forces, the full military (or main force units) and the paramilitary (or guerrilla units), is retained, but priority is assigned to the paramilitary even at the expense of the main force. The quality of the paramilitary must be improved, however, chiefly through increased training and indoctrination and better logistic support. This involves reallocation of resources. It also entails geographic relocation of the war, west to the even more remote areas of the highlands and north to the vicinity of the 17th Parallel. As far as possible, the burden of the war is shifted back to the PLAF forces, and there is less direct PAVN involvement.

¶ The ability of the enemy to initiate battles must be

limited by constantly occupying him and, ideally, confining him to his enclave cities. He must not be permitted to choose the time and place for battle. To accomplish this, dozens if not hundreds of daily small-scale actions must be mounted, either simultaneously or in waves. One's casualties in these actions are not of major consequence, nor is it vital that these engagements end in victory, for even in defeat they serve the objective of pinning down the enemy force, especially the Americans, and closing options for him.

¶ United-front groups must be fully utilized. The GVN's pacification and national development programs must be blunted, sabotaged, frustrated. Control of the villages as sources of supply and manpower must be continued by whatever means necessary. The GVN's effort to break up the NLF organizational structure in the villages must be resisted at all costs.

¶ The DRV-NLF must maximize its already intense externalization program throughout the world, to undercut policy with the American public in the United States and to undermine American diplomacy abroad.

¶ There is a return to emphasis on the Protracted Conflict thesis,[22] especially in South Vietnam. Neorevolutionary Guerrilla War works without a timetable. It has its own peculiar meaning of *victory*, defined as short-term success with long-term impact. Thus it can be asserted that the cause is to be fought as a protracted conflict "achieving decisive victory in a relatively short time."

¶ The struggle must be communicated and portrayed as a national salvation effort, employing the "country saving"

[22] This in itself is not a doctrine, since it does not explain *how* or *why* the PLAF forces are better able to persevere than is the enemy. It simply asserts that this is true. Protracted conflict is the military counterpart to political communism's wave-of-the-future idea.

theme by agit-prop cadres. Above all, it must be pictured as a struggle, not of Vietnamese against Vietnamese (for example, Vietnamese Catholics versus Vietnamese NLF), but of *all* Vietnamese against the foreign invader.

¶ Organization must be such as not to require dependence on the villagers for support. Food, money, shelter, and other requirements may be commandeered, and full coercion is authorized. This would represent no new approach by the NLF. As indicated in Chapter One, the NLF's great strength through the years has been its ability to enmesh the villager in a tightly constructed network of village-control organizations. The cement in this doctrine is the "certainty of victory" propaganda theme. The leadership reasons that it must convince the villager that the NLF will win, that support will then follow regardless of villager attitudes.

¶ More interest in the conference table is found than among the Regular Force strategy advocates. This strategy easily could include the fighting-negotiating idea since what it involves basically is a diminution of conventional war activity; if this could be accomplished on a parity basis through negotiations, it would fit nicely into the Neorevolutionary Guerrilla War strategy.

It should be understood that the nature of this great debate in Hanoi, especially between the Regular Force and the Neorevolutionary schools, is not a well-defined dispute with sharp boundaries and clear-cut positions. Quite the contrary. We are involved here in amorphous argument, with affective utterances on warfare in which it never has been truer that "the letter killeth and the spirit giveth life." For example, Truong Chinh, in the opinion of all Vietnam scholars and experts, is closely and personally associated with the concept of protracted conflict and has been for twenty years.

Yet scattered throughout his writings are paragraphs that read as if they were recent utterances by the Regular Force strategists; passages from *Primer For Revolt* sound like descriptions of the 1968 Tet offensive, which was anything but protracted conflict. The reverse, with General Giap, also is true. His works contain frequent references to protracted conflict, and at times he writes as if he invented the idea. This crossing into the opponent's field is not simply an effort to cover one's flank in a debate. It is that the nature of the debate permits one to absorb many of his opponent's contentions and arguments, even while disputing them.

Negotiated Settlement Strategy. Nguyen Duy Trinh, the "younger elements" of the Politburo,[23] Hoang Van Hoan, Tran Quoc Hoan, and possibly Le Duc Tho advocate a nonmilitary strategy. They argue, in effect, that the objective of unification cannot be achieved by military means, neither by Regular Force nor by Neorevolutionary strategy, and therefore they urge a nonmilitary approach: (*a*) diplomatic efforts between the DRV and other involved parties, but primarily the United States, with the object of getting American *présence* removed from South Vietnam; this can come through Geneva- or Paris-style negotiations or through diplomatic gestures and private signals directly to the United States; (*b*) political efforts in South Vietnam, including negotiations with the GVN, but also united-front activity through the NLF, the Alliance, and, if possible, through other groups such as the militant Buddhists, with the objective of manipulating events in South Vietnam so as to increase DRV influence and control there. By these

[23] Actually younger elements in the Central Committee and upper ranks of the government; there are no young men in the Politburo.

means, it is asserted, Negotiated Settlement becomes a strategy that can yield victory.

In DRV and NLF doctrinal thinking it is important to distinguish between negotiations as a grand strategy and negotiations as a tactic. As a strategy, the negotiator assumes much if not all of the burden of the struggle; that he can do so is questioned by the opponents of the doctrine. As a tactic, negotiations become simply a device to facilitate some other strategy, presumably military, and as such are not opposed doctrinally by anyone. Thus Regular Force and Neorevolutionary Guerrilla War strategy advocates rule out neither tactical negotiations nor nonmilitary efforts in general. Indeed, it is fundamental to all Politburo thinking that the armed struggle and the political struggle must be pursued simultaneously. The quarrel comes over the relative degree of emphasis each is to get, the allocation of resources, or the correct decision to be made in those specific instances (which are frequent) where the interests of one must be served ahead of the interests of the other. General Giap would maintain that while diplomacy abroad and political overtures in the South might make certain limited contributions to his cause, the burden of the struggle must remain military. Truong Chinh and the Neorevolutionary advocates see somewhat greater utility in the conference table than does General Giap, and they suggest a more or less orchestrated effort between guerrilla war and diplomacy politics. But in the final analysis, they would agree with General Giap that victory must be decided in the field, not at the bargaining table or in the political arena in the South. The Negotiated Settlement group would focus the struggle on the nonmilitary, arguing that the military contribution should be almost an attendant holding operation: hold in the field while time runs out for the enemy.

The official and, in general, the actual position of the leading members of the Politburo in Hanoi toward the conference table has been shaped by many forces. But their position is clear. Over the years the DRV leaders have evaluated each proposal for a political settlement — whether it came from U Thant, Pope Paul, or the U.S. State Department — in terms of their fundamental objective, namely unification. In effect, Ho Chi Minh has asked himself of each proposal or offer: *Will it move us, even in a small way, toward unification?* If the answer was yes, then he was interested. If the answer was no, as it was in most cases, then he was not interested. The idea expressed by many onlookers, especially in Europe, that the DRV leaders for some unexplained reason wanted negotiations for the sake of negotiations had no basis in fact. Quite the contrary, the DRV consistently indicated a negative attitude toward the idea of negotiations, of which this was typical:

> The liberation in South Vietnam aims at settling irreconcilable contradictions between our people and imperialism. . . . It is impossible to believe in the peaceful good will of the imperialists or to count on talks and negotiations with them. . . . Particularly with regard to our country it is incorrect. . . . The path of "negotiating" and "becoming reconciled" with and making concessions or "holding hands with the imperialists" is not a path to consolidate peace, nor is it a path to drive back aggression and enslavement in South Vietnam. . . . This revolution can and should be settled only by the use of revolutionary acts and the force of the masses to defeat the enemy forces. It absolutely cannot be settled by laws and accords. . . . Laws and accords consistent with the basic interests of the people and the country can be achieved only through a long, acute struggle of the people against the enemy. . . . It is illusory to hope to persuade the cruel enemy of the people to comply with accords. . . . The contradictions between the people in South Vietnam and the U.S. imperialists and their lackeys are antagonistic. The

correct solution is not to reconcile the contradictions and the classes but through revolution eliminate the contradictions. These contradictions must be settled by an acute life-and-death struggle between ourselves and the enemy. It is impossible to believe in the "peaceful good will" of the imperialists and to count on "talks" and "negotiations" with them. . . . The liberation of South Vietnam can be settled only by force.[24]

The DRV contributions to liberation of the South, however, may be overridden by the long-standing doctrine that building socialism in the North takes priority over all else; it is akin to Stalin's insistence that all the Communist establishment abroad be sacrificed if necessary in defense of the Soviet Union, communism's heartland. Thus negotiations are relevant to DRV internal goals. Nguyen Duy Trinh presents political settlement in terms of building socialism, arguing that it facilitates the effort while military strategies will not. In fact, since most of his life has been spent as an economist rather than a diplomat, probably he argues less from strong faith in political settlement than from a wish to get on with developing the DRV economy, even if it means giving up the goal of unification.

A somewhat different condition has existed with respect to the NLF. In assessing the NLF attitude toward, or behavior during, negotiations, it is vital (though not always possible) to distinguish between DRV-loyal elements in the NLF ostensibly speaking for the organization and the "pure Southern" elements that are still numerically large but not for the most part able to interpret NLF policy. Indigenous Southern elements in the NLF are more amenable to the principle of negotiated settlement than are most of the leaders in Hanoi. This difference in attitude stems from differing objectives: the DRV objective of unification as opposed to the NLF objective of political power. After all,

24 *Hoc Tap,* theoretical Lao Dong Party journal (Hanoi, July 1964).

political power is divisible and thus is responsive to bargaining, unlike unification, which is less subject to compromise.

Several factors thus affect DRV-NLF attitudes toward the conference table. The first is the various objectives, the criterion being whether negotiations serve those objectives.

A second factor in their attitude stems from their assessment of the struggle, that is, whether negotiations are necessary. The Politburo members would argue that if they are going to prevail by military means and if victory is certain, then any negotiations are unnecessary and dangerous. The fortunes of war therefore play a marked role in their thinking. When the tide of war was running sharply with the DRV and NLF in early 1965, they exhibited total indifference to the idea of an international conference on Vietnam (unless, of course, it was to be simply a surrender ceremony). In 1968 when the tide reversed, interest revived, and the Paris meetings opened. However, these "tactical negotiations" are not what is meant by the Negotiated Settlement strategy. The latter is the full route to the objective, the former a means of using the conference table to save or slow a deteriorating situation pending buildup, regrouping, or fielding a new offensive. Certainly nothing indicates that the DRV leaders believe it possible to achieve victory through tactical negotiations, for General Giap would be citing the ancient argument that one cannot win back at the conference table what one has lost on the battlefield.

In the third place, internal politics in the DRV and NLF-PRP, as well as between the Lao Dong and the PRP and the DRV and the NLF, also condition the view of the conference table and activities there. Negotiations affect the political dynamic in the Politburo. They alter the pattern of relationships between Northern and Southern elements. As noted earlier, the Big Five in Hanoi—Ho Chi Minh,

Phan Van Dong, Vo Nguyen Giap, Truong Chinh, and Le Duan—all have opposed the idea of negotiated settlement (as distinguished from tactical negotiations), though for differing reasons and with varying degrees of vehemence. Thus, it is easier to maintain a policy than to switch to a new one. To this fact must be added old-fashioned political vested interest. This issue then—military versus nonmilitary efforts—forms the part of a larger debate in Hanoi, just as the debate itself forms part of the still broader political infighting that goes on there. For some of the DRV officials, such as General Giap, the debate is crucial.

The fourth factor conditioning the DRV leadership's view of negotiated settlement is the virtue syndrome. The men of Hanoi view their cause with profound morality. They see the struggle in terms of good and evil, right and wrong. They are knights who must slay the dragon, not negotiate with him. Anything less than total battle represents a betrayal of high moral values. This is not a pretense, but a genuine attitude, dictating that the pure of heart should win a pure victory, unsullied by contamination or even association with the enemy. The struggle is larger than life, especially in the South, where it is portrayed in ultradramatic terms such as "survival of the Vietnamese people," "preservation of the nation's existence." Because of this view, seating oneself with the enemy seems monstrous.

The fifth factor involves external relations, especially with China. Quite clearly, the Chinese are hostile to the idea of a negotiated settlement. Relations between the DRV and China began deteriorating in early 1968, exacerbated by the DRV decision to begin talks and then negotiations with the United States. The DRV seems willing to allow relations with China to cool, but all evidence indicates that it does not believe in permitting a complete rupture. Peking, for its part, seems willing to tolerate considerable hostility by the DRV providing this does not serve the Soviet Union. As noted earlier, the Chinese touchstone is not the war but the Sino-Soviet dispute.

Finally, the DRV leaders have an irrational distrust if not fear of the conference table. Today's leaders are the same individuals who ruled the DRV during the 1954 Geneva Conference. That meeting haunts them, for they have convinced themselves over the years that they had won all of Vietnam on the battlefield only to lose half of it at the conference table. Indeed, from the leadership's standpoint the 1954 Geneva Conference was a disaster. The DRV's strategy at the Conference was to hold that no military cease-fire agreement could be written until the various political issues were solved, that is, a political settlement reached. In its judgment this was a sound position: assurances, even guarantees, that Vietnam would be united under the Viet Minh banner would be in its hands before the French were let off the hook militarily. From post-Conference data we now know that both the Soviet and the Chinese Communist delegates, dealing separately and secretly with the French, sought to serve their own respective interests and thus circumvented and in the end nullified their Vietnamese ally's bargaining position. Ho Chi Minh lost on every major point: a military cease-fire and what loosely could be called the political settlement occurred simultaneously; the country was divided, and half of it denied him; he was maneuvered out of virtually all leverage then or in the future against the French, and he was alone. The traumatic effect of this loss on the DRV leaders is particularly evident with respect to two negotiational fears: fear of negotiations at premature levels, and fear of negotiations that do not take place at meetings firmly under their control with respect to agenda, participants, and certain other matters.

None of these factors indicates any ideological reason why a negotiated settlement could not be reached. Neither is there any implication that the DRV sees no utility in the conference table. Frequently, especially in internal documents, reference is made to the tactical negotiating of the "fighting-negotiating" concept:

> The idea of fighting-negotiating is not new in our country's history. Nguyen Thai employed such a strategy in defeating feudal elements during the Ming Dynasty. Our comrades in China adopted a fighting-negotiating policy in their struggle against the U.S. and Chiang [Kai-shek]. This strategy also was employed at the end of the Korean war.
>
> However now the matter is complex and the question of negotiations [with the enemy] has developed many divergent views. . . . Some countries which strongly support our struggle want to see us at the conference table, they say, to prevent further needless bloodshed, although their view may result from their own foreign policy considerations, internal politics or misunderstanding of our situation. In our own ranks are those who hold that the political struggle now has become paramount to the military struggle, but the Party view is that at this moment in history this is not true. . . . Negotiation efforts must of course serve the political struggle. Determining the timing of this strategy has been entrusted, by the Party Central Committee voting unanimously, to the Politburo and it will evaluate the situation and the enemy's condition, and determine the proper strategy with respect to negotiations.[25]

Probably a major reason why over the years there has been so little talk in the NLF ranks in the South about negotia-

[25] Letter from Le Duan to General Nguyen Chi Thanh, circa late 1966, published by the Joint U.S. Public Affairs Office, Saigon, Vietnam, under *Vietnam Documents and Research Notes,* No. 8, October 1967.

tions as a route to power is that it tends to undercut zeal on the battlefield. The Paris talks in 1968 presented the NLF with severe disciplinary problems, for all too many PLAF soldiers hearing that "peace" negotiations were underway quite reasonably decided that they did not want to be the last men to die in the war. Therefore, it is common in *kiem thao* and indoctrination sessions to picture negotiations as a tactic. Or they are explained simply as the final act of the drama, delivering the *coup de grâce*.

Negotiations can be viewed as a scale running, say, from 1 to 10. (See Figure 4-1.) At the narrow end, 1 would be single-purpose negotiations (for example, a prisoner exchange: one deal, one time, nothing else discussed); at the broad end of the continuum, 10 would be a full convening of the Geneva Conference (everyone present, the whole future of Indochina to be mapped out). A characteristic of the continuum is that at the narrow end the talks can be bilateral (U.S.-DRV, GVN-DRV, GVN-NLF, etc.), while at the higher end they must be, of necessity, multilateral. The DRV seems willing to negotiate at the narrow end of the spectrum but more reluctant to negotiate at the broad end. Hanoi officials seem to see the March–October 1968 Paris talks, for example, at about Number 3 or 4 on the scale, that is, specific negotiations about American air strikes into North Vietnam; the DRV maintained that it was in Paris to establish a "total, permanent and unconditional halt in American bombing of North Vietnam." At times, Xuan Thuy displayed considerable irritation that the world press continually referred to the talks as "peace negotiations."[26]

[26] Worth noting is the DRV word usage in its domestic accounts of the initial Paris talks. In Vietnamese the word *noi chuyen* means "talks," and its meaning in Vietnamese is as vague as is its English equivalent. Vietnamese has several words for "negotiate," depending on the type of

The complete cessation of American air strikes in the DRV, ordered on November 1, 1968, resulted in moving the negotiations up the continuum scale from the 3 or 4 mark to about 7.

	bilateral	....					multilateral		
1	2	3	4	5	6	7	8	9	10
Vientiane prisoner release		Paris (mid-1968)			Paris (late 1968)				Geneva 1954, 1962
	tactical	....					strategic		

Figure 4-1 Negotiational Spectrum

Certain legal questions are involved in a conference settlement of the Vietnam struggle. The author has delineated these for the benefit of the reader without passing legal judgment.[27] The major aspects involved in taking a judicial view of the Vietnam conflict are these:

1. Are the 1954 Geneva Agreements legally binding on all parties, particularly on the GVN?

The Agreements are not clear in meaning or intent. Not being legal documents in legal language, they are, in key paragraphs, vague and unclear. Thus they can and do mean different things to different persons. The Agreements are in two parts. The first is the *Agreement on Cessation of*

negotiation: *cuoc dam phan* means to negotiate in an informal sense; *thuong luong* means to negotiate in an evaluative or impersonal sense; and *thuong thuyet* means to negotiate in a persuasional sense. In the DRV press in 1968 the term *noi chuyen* was used to describe the talks in Paris; none of the various words for "negotiations" was used.

27 The author is not an international lawyer; in 1967 he attended a week-long academic seminar in Europe on the legal aspects of the Vietnam situation; what appears here is based on his understanding of the various arguments of the sundry international lawyers at the seminar.

Hostilities in Vietnam,[28] dealing with more or less technical aspects of a military cease-fire in the Indochinese War. This was signed by a Viet Minh and a French general and at least is in a legal context. The second document's legality is more questionable. This was the *Final Declaration of the Geneva Conference on the Problem of Restoring Peace to Indochina.* It was not signed by anyone. However, oral subscriptions were offered by Britain, France, the Soviet Union, China, and the Viet Minh (DRV) government, but not by the United States, which issued a separate statement, and of course not by the GVN, which was absent. Since it was neither present nor a "signatory," the GVN position is that the *Final Declaration* is not binding on it, even assuming it is a legal document. It appears that the legal question raised is this: Is an agreement between A and B binding on C when C is not a party to the agreement and in fact, at the time, specifically disassociated himself from the agreement? In civil law the answer quite clearly is that the agreement is not binding on C. Under international law the case is not as clear-cut. Here the question is whether the French, as a colonial power, could make an agreement that would be binding on the "native" government and, further, whether the agreement would continue to be binding upon the transferral of legal sovereignty by the French to the post-colonial government.

Prior to 1954, Vietnam as a state in the French Union did not control its foreign affairs; these were in the realm of the High Council of the French Union, as was the final

[28] It should always be borne in mind that the 1954 Geneva Conference dealt with Indochina rather than simply with Vietnam; in many instances the Conference tended to treat the whole area as a single entity. Technically the Geneva Agreements had three separate accords: Vietnam, Cambodia, and Laos.

power of decision in international obligations. Following the 1954 Geneva Conference, the French withdrew from Vietnam and transferred full control over foreign affairs to the State of Vietnam, called the Republic of Vietnam, that is, South Vietnam. There immediately developed the two-Vietnams problem (see Question 2), namely the DRV and the GVN. The DRV had been in existence since August 1945 as the Viet Minh government and the GVN as a continuation of the Bao Dai government. (Bao Dai himself had been deposed by referendum in late 1955.) Thus the question that arose was whether the now fully independent Republic of Vietnam was responsible for accepting and implementing the Geneva Agreements. There is no unanimity of view among international lawyers on the question of the extent to which a newly independent state is bound by obligations accepted (or forced on it by the colonial power) prior to independence. From a nonlegal practical viewpoint it seems clear that, international law notwithstanding, no ex-colonial nation is going to feel bound to a disadvantageous condition simply because of some document signed by its former colonial master. Such, at least, is the GVN position.

Particularly operative with respect to the Agreement is the matter of elections. The French and the Viet Minh agreed at Geneva that elections would be held in July 1956. In what is a remarkable exercise in semantics, the *Final Declaration* stated that "general elections will be held," *but it did not specify elections for what* — whether they would be elections to choose a single legislature for the entire country, or elections as a referendum on the country's political future, or elections to choose between Ho Chi Minh and Bao Dai–Ngo Dinh Diem, or whatever. It said elections would be held, "in order to insure that sufficient progress in the restoration of peace has been made and that all necessary conditions obtain for expression of the national will."[29] The more often one reads this sentence, the more ambiguous it becomes. The author, at a reception in Saigon in 1960, met casually one of the members of the French delegation of the 1954 Geneva Conference and commented on the superb vagueness of Article Seven of the *Final Declaration,* whereupon the Frenchman seized his hand and said, "Thank you for the compliment, for such was our intention; we stayed up all night phrasing and rephrasing Article Seven." The Cease-fire Agreement makes one reference to elections, in Article Fourteen dealing with political and administrative matters during the cease-fire. It states:

> Pending the general elections which will bring about the unification of Vietnam, the conduct of civil administration in each regrouping zone shall be in the hands of the party whose forces are to be regrouped there in virtue of the present Agreement.[30]

The first twelve words of this paragraph are a sort of *non sequitur* clause, since the article deals not with elections but with technical matters of who will administer the regrouping zones during regrouping. (The agreement is that administration will be handled by whichever side controlled the respective areas at the time of the cease-fire.) In other words, the paragraph deals with administration during a cease-fire and not substantively with the matter of elections.

A further ambiguity is that the *Final Declaration* speaks of elections to result from "consultations to be held on this subject between the competent representative authorities of the two zones" but does not indicate who these competent representative authorities would be. At the time of the

[29] Article Seven of the *Final Declaration.*

[30] Article 14(a) of the *Agreement on the Cessation of Hostilities in Vietnam.*

Geneva Conference, the Viet Minh were the competent representative authority in the North. With the withdrawal of the French, did the GVN become the competent representative authority in the South? If so (to return to the point raised earlier), was the GVN bound by this Agreement? In sum what happened was that the French and the Viet Minh agreed that elections of an unspecified nature would be held in Vietnam, while the Government of South Vietnam declared in effect that they would not take place. Then the French withdrew, and the elections did not take place; the question remained: Was this an illegality?

2. *Legally, are there two Vietnam "states" or only one?*

One view is that Vietnam is a single state temporarily divided against its will (and within this is the question of which government, the GVN or the DRV, if either, is legal). The other major view is that, certainly now and perhaps always, there have been two Vietnam states—the DRV, created in 1945 and granted de facto recognition by the French, and the GVN, which is the legal successor to the Bao Dai monarchy (and through the monarchy a government tracing its heritage back to pre-French days). Under the French, originally, there were three states: Annam, Cochin China, and Tonkin—all part of French Indochina, which also included Laos and Cambodia. Cochin China was a colony, a direct appendage of France. Annam was a monarchy, where the Emperor reigned while the French ruled. In Tonkin the French ruled under a viceroy arrangement. After 1945 there were two governments (but still three states?): the Viet Minh-*cum*-DRV and the Bao Dai–French. At the Geneva Conference the French (again, possibly acting legally for the Bao Dai government) made certain agreements with the DRV, one of which suggested, but did not state, that a single government was to be created, supposedly a new one to incorporate the two present Vietnam governments. The DRV and the GVN each maintains that it is the sole legal government of Vietnam. Some international lawyers take the tack that there are two states in Vietnam neither of which can claim total, permanent sovereignty over all Vietnam, that each of the two states, the GVN and the DRV, is temporarily sovereign in its own sphere, and that the only requirement in the Geneva Agreements (was the conference in a legal position to adjudicate?) is that the two existing states merge into a single new state under conditions acceptable to both. Therefore, according to this argument, both "states" in Vietnam are of a caretaker nature, which legally should pass out of existence upon the creation of a new single state of Vietnam. However, as with the question of whether the agreements are binding on the GVN, we are again faced with the practical fact that seems beyond international law, namely that there are two Vietnams. This may not be legal; it may not be permanent; but for the moment it is a fact.

3. *What is the legal status of the National Liberation Front?*

If the NLF is an authentic indigenous element of the South Vietnamese society, then clearly there exists in Vietnam, legally, a civil war between the GVN and the NLF. This is true whether there is one or two Vietnam "states." If the NLF is not indigenous, then the question arises as to its legal status, whether belligerent, insurgent, or perhaps in some other category. Once it has been defined, the question arises as to whether it has a legal right to participate in a negotiated settlement. It seems clear that if the NLF's origin, composition, direction, and control was and is in the DRV, then it is illegal in South Vietnam and has no standing under international law. But, again, as a practical matter the NLF exists and would be in a position to sabotage any political settlement not acceptable to it.

4. *Does external assistance, by the United States and other non-Communist countries, on the one hand, and by the Communist nations, on the other, constitute an illegal act?* The argument on each side is that each is engaging in collective self-defense measures; this is combined with the assertion that the other side is guilty of aggression. Tangential to this is the question of the degree of legal involvement by outside nations in any settlement. Once again practical aspects seem to be the only germane consideration.

These legal considerations are not, however, the major concern of the Negotiated Settlement strategists. Rather they are interested in the specific mechanics of the effort. Their case may be summarized as follows:

We face two problems: how to get American and other foreign troops out of South Vietnam and how to get into power in Saigon a government that will be amenable to the idea of unification. We cannot drive the Americans out of South Vietnam militarily. The past several years of warfare prove this. Therefore, we must get them out by nonmilitary means. We can do this either by example or by negotiations. In the first instance, we would withdraw PAVN and taper off PLAF combat, hoping that the Americans would begin a withdrawal of their forces. In the second instance, we would negotiate — publicly or secretly — an agreement for the withdrawal of U.S. troops in exchange for whatever we would have to give up as a result of the bargaining. In any case, our calculation is that once out, the Americans will not return. And it is our assumption that once the Americans are out, the prospects are much brighter that a government more sympathetic to us, and to the idea of unification, will come into power in South Vietnam. If not, political forces, or even semi-insurgents, will begin to develop that eventually will be powerful enough to force creation of a government willing to unite with North Vietnam. This may take ten years, or even a generation, but it is bound to succeed in the long run.

What gives this group its importance is its negativism. It argues that present strategies are not working and therefore should be abandoned. But in government the weakest policy position possible is opposition to a program on the grounds that it is a failure, without offering a clear-cut, workable alternative. That one is right, that the policy is a failure, is almost irrelevant. But the group's chief strength, negativism, is also its chief weakness. It cannot prove with certainty that even if the Americans leave South Vietnam, events there in the next decade or generation will necessarily move in the direction of the interests of the DRV.

A capsule description of the three strategies appears in Table 4-1.

An assessment of the doctrinal struggle in Hanoi as of early 1969 was this:

a. That the Regular Force strategists had been so discredited that they no longer enjoyed the support of the majority of the Politburo members.

b. That the members were divided between Neorevolutionary Guerrilla War and Negotiated Settlement strategies.

c. That the final configuration of doctrine would depend partly on events in the other camp (both military and political), partly on the strategy employed by the other camp (the counterpunch gambit), and partly on the outcome of political infighting in Hanoi and in the upper ranks of the NLF.

TABLE 4–1
Summary Comparison of the Three Strategies

	Regular Force Strategy	Neorevolutionary Guerrilla War Strategy	Negotiated Settlement Strategy
Description of strategy	Quick victory, using small-scale and guerrilla war techniques. Great emphasis on logistics. Sudden, massive offensives.	Protracted conflict. Win at Stage Two with modernized guerrilla war tactics. Gnat-swarm warfare.	Achieve victory at the conference table and through political activities in South Vietnam. Guerrilla war makes a contribution.
Protagonists' arguments	A quick victory can be won by launching an ever-greater momentum of attacks, which are militarily and psychologically devastating.	To outlast, outwear, outendure the enemy by military actions that never give him an opportunity to use his vaunted advantages of mass and movement.	It is impossible to drive out the Americans, but it is possible to negotiate them out, or get them out by example of withdrawal of our troops. Once out, they won't come back; once out, whatever else, our prospects will be brighter.
Antagonists' arguments	In a toe-to-toe slugging match the enemy's firepower will decimate our strength, because it is impossible to match his mass and movement.	This is a no-win policy. It permits our forces to continue to survive and exist, but it dooms us never to go through the gates of victory. Slow down a typhoon, and it breaks up.	It is impossible to win at the conference table what cannot be won on the battlefield. The conditions imposed by the enemy for a political settlement would be disadvantageous, if not disastrous.

TABLE 4–1 (continued)

	Regular Force Strategy	Neorevolutionary Guerrilla War Strategy	Negotiated Settlement Strategy
Relevancy of logistics and outside support	Maintain maximum effort to sustain highest levels; match the enemy. Major outside logistic assistance required.	Opposed to symmetrical escalation; keep logistic demands to a minimum; be self-contained, self-supporting. Minimum outside assistance required.	Logistics and manpower demands low; less strain on all systems as a result.
View of time	Time not on our side. Must compress events in time.	Time is our best ally. War is a test of wills, a dimension of time.	Time inevitably will be with us; the force of haste will chiefly be in the other camp.
View of negotiations	Negotiate only a diminution of the enemy's military advantages (in firepower or manpower). Tactical negotiations permissible.	Negotiate to diminish the level or magnitude of the war. Tactical negotiations permissible.	Negotiate all, chiefly at strategic level.
Advocates of strategy	Vo Nguyen Giap; Ho Chi Minh; Van Tien Dung, Le Duan; "hardliners" in NLF.	Truong Chinh; Le Thanh Nghi, Pham Hung, Le Duc Tho (?); certain professional (nonmilitary) PAVN generals; the Chinese Communists; the few remaining original NLF cadres.	Nguyen Duy Trinh, Hoang Van Hoan, Tran Quoc Hoan; the "younger elements" of Lao Dong Central Committee; Southern elements of the NLF.

d. That Ho Chi Minh particularly would seek a doctrinal compromise that would placate if not satisfy all Politburo members. Most likely this would involve both serious political settlement efforts and lower-level but still intensive guerrilla warfare.

CHAPTER FIVE

PROSPECTS AND POTENTIALS

I shall conclude with a cautious look at Vietnam's prospects in the short run, that is, the next ten years or so, and its potential for the long run, the next generation. The struggle in Vietnam is what the academic gamesters call a zero-sum game, like poker, in which what one player wins the others must lose, and it all must total zero. The problem in Vietnam since 1954 has been how to convert the situation to a non-zero-sum game. It seems to me that men are limited in this effort, but that eventually time will do the job for them.

Short-Range Prospects

The short-range prospects are for a gradual shifting of effort and attention from military to nonmilitary activities, the reduction of warfare, and the intensification of diplomacy abroad and politics in South Vietnam.

Military disengagement, the physical separation of the contending forces, eventually will come in Vietnam probably by a combination of negotiations, tacit agreements, and unilateral decisions. Both sides will label this victory — claims that should not ruffle us too much. The first step in this disengagement must be a diminution of the magnitude of the war, which will come only when each party sees such a diminution in its interest. This could be the first step toward private accommodation. In any event, it will result in (or be the result of) a change of strategy by Hanoi. No one can put a time frame on this disengagement, but it will come.

The dynamics of the military scene will, of course, remain. But it is probable that bloodshed will continue though at a lesser rate. Reduction in the level of the war will place internal strains on both camps by triggering debates over the wisdom of the new strategy, especially in Hanoi, where stark doctrinal positions exist. Ironically, as relations within the Politburo in Hanoi worsen, DRV-GVN relations could improve slightly as the cooling-off period that accompanies and follows disengagement begins to heal the wounds of war. The onlooking world will probably see all this chiefly in such verbal shorthand terms as "serious, significant talks," the "fighting-negotiating period," *quid pro quo* reduction of the war's level, symmetrical troop withdrawal, item-by-item mutual or reciprocal de-escalation, reverse tit-for-tat syndrome, or whatever new terminology is coined by the pundits. The degree of success obtainable at the conference table remains problematical. The author is on the side of the pessimists, not by nature, but as a result of eight years in Vietnam. Although fighting will continue at a reduced level and both sides will feel free to make their military strikes, both will seek victories to enhance and strengthen their bargaining position, neither will take such military action as to jeopardize the negotiations themselves. Gradually the war will fade, although it seems probable that 1980 will still find guerrillas in attacks.

It is likely that most of the action in the next decade will come, with ever-increasing momentum, in the nonmilitary sphere. The confrontation will be political in South Vietnam. The NLF and DRV will maintain an undiminished psychological attack on the GVN and its armed forces. The South Vietnamese governing structure must find a way to counter this. It must continue to broaden its political base and to develop a government that is rational, efficient, and attractive to the populace. Unless it ends the existing political disarray, it loses all.

The struggle will, undoubtedly, be more with the NLF than with the DRV and more in the rural areas than in the cities. Accommodation of the dissident (but non-DRV) elements in South Vietnam on a fair-share basis must continue to be the basic policy of the GVN. Eventually this may involve direct GVN-NLF negotiations. But for the most part it will be a political struggle (though sometimes with guns) against the NLF organs in the arena of the country's 2,500 villages. For the NLF this will be the most deadly battle of all, with nothing less than its survival at stake. The organization weapon is to be tested at Armageddon. The struggle will be silent, unspectacular, and largely beyond the comprehension of outsiders. The prospect is that the NLF will move from the defensive to the beleaguered. The Workers' Liberation Association cadres increasingly will be challenged by the trade-union organizers from Saigon. The Farmers' Liberation Association will discover that its members are listening to the call of farm and fishing cooperative leaders in provincial capitals. The Youth Liberation Association and the Student Liberation Association will be picked apart by a swarm of youth and student groups, some Buddhist, some Catholic, some sectarian, some left-wing, some right-wing, some center, some highly idealistic, some candidly mercenary—all attacking with the untiring zeal that marks anything done by the young. The NLF will be pursued through the jungle by the pack.

The parameters of this political struggle are hard to discern. Certainly a chief characteristic will be organization versus counterorganization. The NLF will continue to control certain areas of rural Vietnam although, as noted before, the rural area as a whole will continue to decline in importance as the urban-rural ratio rises above its present 50-50 level. Some Vietnamese predict the "unofficial partition" of South Vietnam into NLF-dominated and GVN-controlled areas, the so-called Swiss Cantonment thesis. Like the idea of a cease-fire, the chief argument against this thesis is the sheer complexity of it. The NLF will tend to fragment into a decentralized, modified warlord arrangement. Private armies have long been common in South Vietnam, and we may expect them to proliferate on both sides. The GVN itself has underway a new "civil defense" scheme that seeks to create still another layer of organized, armed Vietnamese below the militia (the Popular Force and the Regional Force), which in turn is below the armed forces. We must not forget, either, that Vietnam is a society in which loyalties are less at the national level than at lower geographic levels, or that the government in Saigon itself is a coalition of mutual-interest protective associations.

Powerful undercurrents are beginning to flow in South Vietnam. One senses the start of a sea change in the Vietnamese people's attitude toward their nation, their society, and the war. A perceptive South Vietnamese military officer, General Duong Van Minh, illustrated this new current of thought in his confession of Vietnamese mistakes in recent years:

Our biggest mistake was to have gone too fast when we

should have gone slow and to have gone too slow when we should have gone fast. . . .

Our next biggest mistake was to place loyalty to self, to family, to friends ahead of loyalty to nation. . . .

Another mistake which so many of the South Vietnamese made was to embrace the illusion that they could somehow stand apart from the conflict, disassociating themselves from both their government and the communists, while giving lip service to either side as the occasion required.[1]

Long-Range Potentials

Oddly, one can answer the question of where Vietnam will be a generation from now with a somewhat greater feeling of certitude than the question of where will it be next year. This final section is not intended as a crystal-ball gazing but rather a summary of the points made earlier to suggest the long-range direction.

The basis of this projection rests on two facts that seem indisputable, one involving a philosophy of history, the other involving the developing relationships among Asian nations.

The first is the fact of change. As we move into the next generation, Vietnam will face the inexorable law of history — that all things change, that nothing is immutable, that this too shall pass away. We do not know the nature of this change; we know only that it will come. We cannot predict the sort of government that will exist in Hanoi a generation from now; but whatever it is, it will not be today's. Neither will there be the same leaders nor the same motivating ideas nor the same values. This, of course, is equally true in South Vietnam. Therefore in considering the Vietnam po-

[1] Duong Van Minh, "A Question of Confidence," *Foreign Affairs*, Vol. 47, No. 1 (October 1968).

tential, we must think in terms of tomorrow's materials, not today's conditions.

The second fact is that regionalism is a major force of the future in Asia. The dream of internationalism has faded, at least for the moment, and we are further from a one-world government than we were twenty years ago. This too will change, since world government seems inevitable in the very long run, that is, in terms of centuries; but in our lifetime we can expect associational emphasis to be regional, not international. A great deal of regionalism, though in its infancy, is already underway in Southeast Asia and in Asia in general. This is not simply collective military efforts, such as SEATO, but a whole host of regional arrangements.[2]

In Vietnam the force of change and the drive of regionalism will, in all likelihood, move Vietnam and other countries in Indochina toward confederation. A generation from now probably we will see the creation and full fruition of a Federation of Indochina, composed of two Vietnams, Laos, and Cambodia. Possibly some day the Federation might also include Thailand. This Federation of Indochina would be federal, and the internal sovereignty and security of each

2 The first significant articulation of which came in April 1947 when Jawaharlal Nehru convened the Asian Relations Conference. Other milestones: Burma's call in 1949 for a regional defense organization (turned down by all parties, including the United States); the 1953 Asian Socialist Conference; the 1955 Afro-Asian Conference in Bandung; the stillborn Maphilindo (grouping of the Philippines, Malaysia, and Indonesia); the Asian Pacific Council (ASPAC) (Australia, Nationalist China, Japan, South Korea, Malaysia, New Zealand, the Philippines, Thailand, and South Vietnam, with Laos as an observer); and the Association of Southeast Asian Nations (ASEAN) (Indonesia, Philippines, Malaysia, and Thailand). The U.N.'s Economic Commission for Asia and the Far East (ECAFE), the Colombo Plan, and of course the Southeast Asia Treaty Organization (SEATO) represent regional group cooperation with outside powers.

member would be respected by all others, as well as guaranteed by all others. Specifically, this would mean an understanding that no member engages in internal subversion against other members. It would succeed only if each member found more value in federation than in the possibilities of subversion or invasion. Understandably, the Federation would at the start be a loose grouping with weak institutions. Probably it would begin with a common market, economic barter deals, creation of common currency, common passports, and so on, gradually working toward the more sensitive areas.

The framework of the Federation of Indochina would be the means (or the scenario, in modern academic parlance) for a gradual joining together of North and South Vietnam, unification, but by peaceful, noncoercive, nonsubversive, and mutually beneficial means. Vietnam would thus be unified, but the unification would not mean the same thing as it does now because it would be part of a broader context. A non-zero-sum game would be created. The DRV would get what it wants: unification. The GVN would get what it wants: internal security, reaffirmation of its sovereignty, and a chance to engage in national development. Outside parties such as the United States would get what they want: maintenance of stability and equilibrium in Asia and reassertion of the principle that there ought not to be any change on the international level by force.[3] To a large degree the "negotiator" would be time. Both DRV and NLF spokesmen in past interviews, when asked about the timetable for unification (their style), stressed that the process would be time-consuming, that it would be carried out by stages, and would of necessity be a lengthy process. The GVN, for its

[3] As described earlier, the U.S. position is that it is not against unification of Vietnam but against unification by force or subversion.

part, has repeatedly said that it stands ready to explore with DRV officials the question of unification by peaceful means. For example, President Thieu, following the 1968 Honolulu Conference, declared:

> When peace is restored, the Government of Vietnam is ready to explore with the authorities in North Vietnam all the avenues that may lead to the reunification of the country by peaceful means, through free and democratic choice of all Vietnamese in the North and in the South. Pending actual reunification, the gradual normalization of economic, cultural, and family relations between North Vietnam and South Vietnam can be usefully explored. This is an issue that can be decided only by a common accord between the Government of Vietnam and the authorities now in control of North Vietnam.[4]

What these respective positions indicate is that time is available for unification. Of course, it would have to be a coming together freely, under parity, without internal subversion by either party, and to the mutual benefit of both.

The foreign policy of the Federation of Indochina probably would lean toward the neutralist position. Such would be in the interest of the Federation, just as it would be in the interest of non-Communist nations in the Pacific area to "defuse" Indochina and move it out of the Cold War or struggle-for-power context. This would mean withdrawal of all foreign troops, of course. One Pacific power, China, would disapprove of a Federation of Indochina, whatever its foreign policy. China would not like to see 45 million Indochinese, all with a historic antipathy to her, bound together. To what extent she would go to prevent federation is problematical. But just as time works its change elsewhere,

[4] President Nguyen Van Thieu, television broadcast over Television Saigon, August 23, 1968.

so it will with China. It does not seem excessively optimistic to believe that in the next generation China's neuroses will diminish, that she will develop a sense of her own limitations, particularly internal, and will become more realistic (live and let live) in her attitude toward her neighbors. American relations with China probably will move gradually from increased contacts to *détente* to more or less normal relations.

Another major long-run potential is the fading of existing ideological differences between North and South Vietnam. Although great gulfs do exist and the hostility level is unbelievably high, it is for the most part visceral, not ideological. The North Vietnamese are dedicated and loyal people who think they are Communists, that is, Marxist-Leninists, but are so only by their own definition. Hanoi's brand of communism is not communism by Moscow's standards, although Moscow has chosen never to make a point of this. The author has talked to many North and South Vietnamese prisoners, defectors, and *hoi chanh* who were members of the Lao Dong or PRP, but who in conversation denied the following: (1) that the "history of all hitherto existing societies is the history of the class conflict"; (2) that inevitably one epoch is transformed into another, that capitalism gives way to socialism, which phases into communism (most say they believe this will happen but do not see it as an *inevitable* process); (3) that tools of production, whether industrial or agricultural, must be "socialized," that is, industries nationalized and farms collectivized (most are opposed to land collectivization); (4) that communism is antireligious and that religion is the opiate of the people (most deny Marx ever claimed it was). Now if one does not believe in the class conflict doctrine, in historical determinism, or in abolition of private property, then one is not a

Communist as the term is used in the West. Yet these same people said they had been willing (and some still were) to die for communism. They admitted knowing nothing of the subject (few had ever read Marx, Lenin, Stalin, or even Mao Tse-tung), and furthermore they denied that reading was necessary; as several expressed it: *it is not necessary to know anything about communism to be a good Communist.* Contrast this to Western communism. To the Vietnamese, communism is an icon to hang on the wall, a symbol of something to fight and die for, but not something to study and understand. To a Russian or Western Communist, communism is a body of knowledge, something to be absorbed and mastered, a valuable tool that, if one fully masters it, yields infallibility, which obviously is an advantage in contests with non-Communists. The point here is that the "sacred" communism of Vietnam is not a barrier to federation as would be the case with "secular" communism facing federation elsewhere. The idea, for example, of a federation of Austria, Hungary, Switzerland, and Czechoslovakia is not only absurd but technically unworkable. Nothing would mesh — neither the patterns of thought, nor the institutions, nor the definitions of where society ought to go or how it ought to get there. Such is not the case in Asia, particularly Vietnam, where the problem is not the merger of two distinct sociopolitical systems but coexistence between two divergent religions. Over the long run — and it should be stressed again that we are concerned with conditions approaching the year 2000 — the icon of communism will remain in North Vietnam but will determine behavior even less than it does today. North Vietnam may retain some of its ambitions, but these will be more nationalistic than communistic.

The economic system of the Federation of Indochina

probably will be socialist, with considerable agrarian "capitalism." This too will not be incompatible in North Vietnam. It is likely that the economic base will be agrarian rather than industrial. All four of the potential members have an abundance of rich farm land and no overpopulation problem (the reverse of much of the rest of Asia) and therefore presumably will capitalize on these advantages by stressing agricultural development rather than industrialization, to become the rice basket of Asia. Since no Communist nation anywhere has satisfactorily solved its agricultural problem, and since the improvements that have been made (as in Yugoslavia) are the result of moving away from communism on the farm, it is reasonable to believe that these forces will continue to undermine Marxism-Leninism in North Vietnam at least with respect to crop production. Thus nationalism and regionalism will pull on the DRV politically, while private-sector farming will pull on it economically. (There would be other economic lures as well, for example, joint economic ventures such as the enormously ambitious Mekong River Basin plan, to which the United States has pledged a billion dollars.) In short, the idea of confederation, which would be ridiculous elsewhere, is sound in Indochina. This is not to say that it will actually take place but simply to suggest that it is feasible.

Yet I believe, with more conviction than proof, that we shall see some day the emergence of a Federation of Indochina. Within its framework will be found answers to now insoluble problems. Old animosities will be dissipated and lost. New opportunities will emerge that never existed before. The whole will vastly exceed the sum of the parts. Most of all, to me, the Vietnamese people can at last begin to travel on the high road to peace, happiness, and the good life of which fate has cheated them for so long. A Federation of

Indochina can be a new order of things, infinitely brighter a sun, that almost will be worth the agony of the war: "The symbolic bird of Vietnam is the Phoenix and like the Phoenix, Vietnam has throughout its history risen again and again from the ashes . . . and from its own internal mistakes, to become a stronger, wiser people."[5]

[5] Duong Van Minh, *op. cit.*

NAME INDEX

SUBJECT INDEX